QUARTER CENTENNIAL.

TWENTY-FIFTH ANNIVERSARY

OF THE

ORGANIZATION OF THE

FIRST CONGREGATIONAL CHURCH

OF

DETROIT, MICHIGAN.

DECEMBER 8TH, 9TH AND 10TH, 1869.

"*For with my staff I passed over this Jordan, and now I am become two bands.*" — GEN. xxxii: 10.

DETROIT:
TRIBUNE BOOK AND JOB OFFICE.
1870.

CHURCH OFFICERS

FOR A QUARTER CENTURY.

PASTORS AND ACTING PASTORS.

Henry L. Hammond, ...	1844 — 1847
Harvey D. Kitchel, D.D., . . .	1848 — 1864
Samuel M. Freeland, ...	1864 — 1866
Addison Ballard, D.D., ...	1866 — ——

DEACONS.

Sherman S. Barnard, ...	1845 — ——
Charles Howard, ...	1845 — 1861
Silas M. Holmes, ...	1849 — 1861
Francis Raymond, ...	1856 — ——
Lyman Baldwin, ...	1856 — ——
Charles I. Walker, ...	1861 — 1865
William Warner, ...	1861 — 1865
Timothy L. Partridge, ...	1865 — 1868
Charles I. Walker, ...	1866 — ——
Charles E. Silsbee, ...	1866 — 1866
Henry E. Bostwick, ...	1868 — ——
Henry E. Baker, ...	1868 — ——

CLERK.

Francis Raymond, ...	1844 — ——

SUPERINTENDENTS OF THE SUNDAY SCHOOL.

Charles Howard, ...	1845 — 1849
Orrin C Thompson, ...	1849 — 1851
Charles S. Cushing, ...	1851 — 1855
Henry E. Baker, ...	1855 — 1860
Robert W. King, ...	1860 — 1864
Edwin C. Hinsdale, ...	1864 — 1866
Robert W. King, ...	1866 — 1868
Henry E. Bostwick, ...	1868 — ——

THE

ANNIVERSARY PROCEEDINGS.

At a meeting of the First Congregational Church and Society, held June 14, 1869, it was resolved, after full consideration, to celebrate in a becoming manner the Twenty-Fifth Anniversary of the organization of the Church, and, to this end, ROBERT W. KING, HENRY E. BAKER, WILLIAM C. HOYT, EDWIN C. HINSDALE, CHARLES I. WALKER, WILLIAM A. BUTLER and FRANCIS RAYMOND were appointed a Committee of Arrangements, with power to fix upon and carry out such a programme as, in their judgment, should most fitly commemorate the event. This Committee organized by choosing ROBERT W. KING as its Chairman and FRANCIS RAYMOND as its Secretary. It was decided that the celebration should occupy the evenings of three days, and, inasmuch as the actual date of the anniversary to be observed fell upon Christmas Day, it was resolved to fix upon a time midway between the date of the first preliminary meeting looking to the organization of the church and the period of its actual organization. Accordingly, December 8, 9 and 10 were chosen, and it was further determined that, on the first evening, a Historical Address and an Anniversary Poem should be delivered; on the second evening, there should be a general reunion of all former and present members and invited friends; and, on the third evening, a Memorial Address concerning deceased members should be delivered. It was then resolved to invite Hon. CHARLES I. WALKER to deliver the Historical Address, and Rev. HARVEY D. KITCHEL, D.D., the Memorial Address, and these invitations were accepted by the gentlemen named. The latter requested a modification of the Committee's plan so far as to allow him to confine his commemorative discourse to the period beginning with the founding of the church, and closing with the termination of his pastorate in 1864, leaving to his successors the duty of speaking of those whose decease occurred during their ministry. This change was accordingly made, and Rev. SAMUEL M. FREELAND and Rev. ADDISON BALLARD, D.D., were requested to prepare Memorial Addresses also, covering the period of their pastorates, which they did. Mrs. JULIA P. BALLARD was also invited to prepare an Anniversary Poem. It was further determined to invite all the old members of the church, removed to other communions, to join in the proposed celebration, as also to extend a like invitation to all the Congregational ministers in this State, and their wives. Recognizing the value and large importance of the faithful and earnest services of Rev. HENRY L. HAMMOND, and his brother, Hon. CHARLES G. HAMMOND, rendered to the Church in the early years of its struggles for an existence, it was resolved to extend to them a special invitation to be present with us in celebrating the close of a quarter century in the laborious beginnings of which they had so honorable a share.

In accordance with the general programme above set forth, the church, with a goodly number of its invited guests, assembled in the spacious audience room of its house of worship, which had been most elaborately and beautifully trimmed with evergreens and flowers, on Wednesday evening, December 8th, the Pastor, Rev. Dr. BALLARD, presiding. After the singing of an anthem by the choir, an invocation was offered, and a selection from the Scriptures read, by Rev. H. L. HUBBELL, of Ann Arbor. This was followed by the singing of the following hymn, written for the occasion, by Mrs. JULIA P. BALLARD:

O Thou, whose ever-listening ear
Thy children's faintest cry doth hear,
Thy gracious love to us impart,
Great Helper of each waiting heart.

Be with us while, as one, we meet
Thy special mercies to repeat;
While we our song of praise renew,
"The Lord hath helped us hitherto."

The past Thy tender care hath found,
The present with Thy love is crowned;
Let all the future work Thy will,
The Lord shall be our Helper still.

Prayer was then offered by Rev. O. C. THOMPSON, who was the minister earliest connected in anywise with the church, after which the hymn beginning

"O God of Bethel! by whose hand"

was sung. Rev. Dr. BALLARD then delivered the following Address of Welcome:

BRETHREN AND FRIENDS—We are met, this evening, to celebrate the Twenty-Fifth Anniversary of the Organization of our Church and Society.

We feel that the results of that organization have been so good, so great, and so abiding, that we are abundantly justified in giving to the event this public commemoration. As Moses turned aside to behold the bush burning, yet unconsumed, so do we feel that it is worth pausing a while to consider the origin and history of the Church of Jesus Christ, which has firmly maintained its place for a quarter of a century, and which survives in vigor amid the wasting hostilities of such a world as this.

But apart from that, we are drawn to this celebration by a sweet feeling of affectionate gratitude. We who have drank of these refreshing waters, love to trace the stream of blessing back to its source. We love, in this emphatic way, to tell those who founded this church how great and good a work they did, and to thank them for doing it. THE EARLY FOUNDERS — we welcome you, first of all, to taste these harvest-fruits of a field which you enclosed and first planted. We extend a joyful greeting to the former PASTORS of this church. We thank them for all their earnest, patient and successful labors here. Brethren who have stood before me in this office, and especially you, my brother,* who for so many years ministered at this altar, and in these homes, hundreds of hearts turn with tender love to you to-night.

We welcome most cordially those who, obeying the impulses of an honorable Christian enterprise, and led, as we believe, by the Providence and Spirit of God, went out from us a few years since to form a new rallying post for the army of our Immanuel.

We welcome back warmly all the former members of this church and congregation. We welcome the pastors who have come from different parts of the State to share in and increase our joy; as, also, the pastors who represent other Churches of Christ in the city.

We welcome all of our fellow citizens who have come in to see us and to lend us the encouragement of their friendly presence.

We heartily welcome you to our hearts, to our homes, to our sanctuary, to a share with us in this our glad Feast of Remembrance and of Thanksgiving. Together we will recall the loving kindness of our God in the midst of His temple.

---

*Alluding to Rev. Dr. KITCHEL.

The Historical Address was next read by E. C. HINSDALE, Esq., sudden and serious illness preventing Judge WALKER, the Historian, from participating in the anniversary celebration. At the close of the address, which, though occupying a full hour and a half in its reading, was listened to with the strictest attention, Rev. P. R. HURD of Romeo, offered a fervent prayer. This was followed by the reading of the Commemorative Poem, written by Mrs. JULIA P. BALLARD, by R. W. KING, Esq. "Shining Shore" was then sung, and the benediction, pronounced by Rev. Dr. KITCHEL, dismissed the assembly.

On Thursday evening, the general reunion of the old and present members of the church, together with invited guests, took place, and was well attended. Rev. Dr. BALLARD presided, and an introductory prayer was offered by Rev. WILLIAM PLATT of Utica. After a few prefatory remarks by the Pastor, brief and interesting addresses were made by Rev. O. C. THOMPSON, Mr. ISRAEL COE, now of Newark, N. J., and one of the earliest members of the church, Rev. Dr. KITCHEL, Rev. S. M. FREELAND, and Rev. W. P. RUSSELL of Memphis. These were followed by cordial congratulatory and fraternal addresses from representatives of the other denominations of the city, Rev. A. T. PIERSON, of the Fort Street Church, speaking in behalf of the Presbyterians, and Rev. A.

OWENS, of the Lafayette Avenue Church, for the Baptists. Unable to be present in person, Rev. F. A. BLADES, Presiding Elder of the Detroit District, Methodist Church, sent a very hearty and earnest letter on behalf of his denomination. Concluding addresses were then made by CHARLES A. KENT, Esq., and Rev. A. S. KEDZIE, of Dexter. The audience then adjourned to the lecture room where an elegant collation, prepared by the ladies of the church, was served, and the remainder of the evening was spent in most agreeable social intercourse.

On Friday evening, the concluding exercises of this anniversary occasion took place. After an opening anthem by the choir, the hymn beginning

"Let Saints below in concert sing"

was sung, followed with reading the Scriptures and prayer by Rev. J. S. HOYT of Port Huron, and the singing of the hymn

"Jerusalem, my glorious home,"

Rev. Dr. KITCHEL, then delivered his Memorial Address, and was followed by Rev. S. M. FREELAND and Rev. Dr. BALLARD, the latter closing with an earnest exhortation to the renewed and more faithful consecration of those present to the service of the Master, admonished as they were by the solemn recitals of the evening, of the shortness of life and the certainty of death. "Whatsoever thy hand findeth to do, do it with thy might; for there is no work, nor device, nor knowledge, nor wisdom, in the grave, whither thou goest." And then, after singing, "Shall we gather at the River?" a benediction, which was a commendation of all to the sure mercies and sufficient grace of a covenant-keeping God, was pronounced by Rev. Dr. KITCHEL, and the celebration of the first Quarter-Centennial of the church was at an end.

HISTORICAL ADDRESS,

BY

HON. CHARLES I. WALKER,

OF DETROIT.

ADDRESS.

Twenty-five years ago to-night there gathered in the old City Hall, then dimly lighted by oil lamps, about a dozen persons, who there took the first steps towards organizing this church. The hall was then used as a Circuit Court room, and was also a place for all kinds of public gatherings. It was, as now, difficult of access, illy kept, and uninviting.

The Rev. HENRY L. HAMMOND presided over that gathering, and SAMUEL COIT, now of Hartford, was Secretary. A committee, consisting of S. S. BARNARD, ISRAEL COE, CHARLES G. HAMMOND, JAMES G. CRANE and WILLIAM COOK, was appointed to prepare and report a Confession of Faith and Rules of Practice for the church, which it was then proposed to organize. The committee wisely adopted the Confession of Faith of the First Presbyterian Church and reported the same evening, and their report was adopted. A committee was also appointed to call a Council to consider the propriety of organizing a Congregational Church in this city.

This Council met on the 25th of December following, and the result was the organization of this church.

DETROIT AS IT WAS IN 1844.

To form a proper estimate of the enterprise thus originated, it is essential that we know what Detroit then was. It had partaken largely of the causes and results of the financial revulsion of 1837—a revulsion more sudden, severe and long continued, than any other known to our history. It is difficult for any one not personally familiar with that period to form any correct idea of the wild spirit of speculation that prevailed in the country, and particularly in this State, previous to the suspension of specie payments in 1837, or of the utter and wide-spread financial ruin that succeeded that event,—a ruin made more complete in this State by a disastrous system of fraudulent banking that here prevailed. Before the period of which we now speak, the banks had nearly all utterly failed, and a large proportion of our business men had either become bankrupt, or so embarrassed and crippled in their resources, as to paralyze their business energies. For the most part, there was absolutely no market for real estate, and hundreds of thousands of acres of valuable lands had been abandoned by the owners, who chose this course rather than pay the taxes thereon. The State, too, of which Detroit was then the Capital, was literally bankrupt; so much so, that in 1843 the Legislature was paid off by warrants upon an empty treasury, which were hawked about the streets at a large discount.

The city which had, in 1830, a population of two thousand two hundred and twenty-two, increased rapidly till the crisis came, and real estate commanded enormous prices. From that time to 1840, its population decreased, and it then numbered nine thousand one hundred and fourteen. In September, 1844, the number, by actual count, was ten thousand nine hundred and forty-eight. The crisis of depression had then passed, and the prospect for the future was somewhat more hopeful. The city then extended from Dequindre street on the east, to Fourth street on the west; but a very large proportion of this territory was without streets or buildings, save a few scattered farm houses. The whole number of streets, lanes, and alleys, that bore names, was only sixty-five. Not one of these streets was then paved, and there were seasons when they were almost impassable. As yet there were few private carriages, and no public ones, save hotel omnibuses. The most wealthy of the inhabitants still indulged in French carts and, on Sunday, an array of them might be seen on Woodward avenue, extending from Congress to Larned streets, backed up against the sidewalk, awaiting the forthcoming of their aristocratic proprietors from the Presbyterian and Episcopalian churches. Gas had not yet been introduced.

East of this place, there was no railroad nearer than Buffalo, but a daily line of stages left the city for the east by way of Toledo, the Black Swamp and Northern Ohio, and at times, for weeks together, the travel was almost entirely suspended, from the impassable character of the roads. A tri-weekly stage left the city for Port Huron. The Michigan Central road had just been completed to Marshall, and was traversed by one train of coaches each way per day. It was owned by the State, and the depot was on Michigan avenue, where the new City Hall now is. The Detroit & Pontiac R. R. had been completed to Pontiac the preceding year, and, without any passenger depot, received and discharged its passengers by the side of Andrews' Hotel, where the Opera House now stands. Neither of these roads was connected by rail with the river. None of the plank roads, which subsequently opened to us the interior of the State, had yet been built.

West of our own State, there were no railroads. The Illinois Central and the Northwestern railroads, with their wonderful net-work of connections, were not yet in existence, and the Pacific road was but a dream of the far-distant future.

Where the Merrill Block now stands, on the corner of Jefferson and Woodward avenues, there was a two-story brick building known as Smart's Block. Between that block and the National Hotel, now forming the north wing of the Russell House, except the Episcopalian church and the Presbyterian church and session room, there were no structures of brick. From the Labadie-Campau corner (Smith's Jewelry store) to Campus Martius there were no brick stores, save the low three-story block adjoining Campbell & Linn's. Beyond the Campus Martius there were few buildings of any kind, and only one of brick, situated at the corner of Farrar and State streets, which was built for a Methodist church, but was then occupied as a theater. The best brick block in the town was the Eldred Block, on Jefferson avenue, adjoining Smith's Jewelry store. The most expensive private residence was that of Theo. Romeyn, Esq., on the corner of Fort and Wayne streets, now occupied by Mr. J. R. Grout; and next to that in cost was the new brick residence of Robert Stuart, then Superintendent of Indian Affairs, situated on Jefferson avenue, so long and so recently occupied by his family.

There were at that time eleven Church organizations in the city. Of these, three were Catholic, and were served by a Bishop and six Priests. St. Ann's was the oldest and had the largest attendance, as the French population was principally Catholic, and then formed a very large proportion of the inhabitants of our city. This Church dates its origin from the time of De la Motte Cadillac, the founder of Detroit. The present building was commenced in 1817. There were, at the time, two other Catholic Churches. That of the Holy Trinity occupied a wooden building upon the corner of Bates street and Michigan Grand avenue, the present site of Schultheis' marble shop. The building was originally the Fiist Presbyterian church, and when, in 1834, the brick church then standing was erected, this was removed to the place named, and subsequently to the 8th Ward. St. Mary's, German Catholic, church, upon the corner of Croghan and St. Antoine streets, was commenced in 1841, and was still unfinished, but had been used for worship since 1843. The corner stone of the Cathedral on Jefferson avenue was laid June 29th, of this same year, 1844, but as yet little progress had been made thereon. At this time, the majority of the population of the city were Roman Catholics, who numbered probably from six to seven thousand.

The oldest, most numerous, wealthy and influential Protestant organization was the First Presbyterian Church, or, as its corporate name was, the First Protestant Society. This Society was informally organized in August, 1816, and the Rev. JOHN MONTEITH, who reached here the June preceding, became its minister. In 1818, a Church was organized *Presbyterial* in its character, but not *Presbyterian*, and nearly the entire Protestant population, for a time, joined in its support. On the 23d of January, 1825, it re-organized and became distinctly a Presbyterian Church. The building stood upon the corner of Larned street and Woodward avenue, where Nall's store now stands, and was of brick, eighty feet by one hundred, having cost about twenty-five thousand dollars. The Society also had a brick session room immediately north of the church. Rev. Dr. DUFFIELD was then pastor, and the membership was about four hundred. The congregation was very large.

Next, in point of age, was the Methodist Church, which was organized in March, 1822. There had been Methodist preaching in Detroit at a very early day, which was continued with some interruptions to the time mentioned. *Before* the war of 1812, and perhaps *after* that war, there was a small Church here, but the organization of that denomination, existing in 1844, bears the date I have mentioned. The church was a wooden building standing upon the corner of Congress street and Woodward avenue, where Gunn & Locke's store now is, and the same building is now used as a Methodist church on the corner of Lafayette avenue and Fourth streets. They then had about two hundred and eighty members. A second Church was organized in September, 1843, and, at the time we speak of, consisted of sixty members, and met in the United States Court room, the building now occupied by the First National Bank. This Society afterwards completed the Congress Street Methodist church, and worshiped there until they united with the Woodward Avenue Church, constituting the present Central Church. There was also a colored Methodist Church, which was organized in 1836, and consisted at this time of seventy-six members, and met in a building formerly occupied by the Territorial Council on East Fort street.

St. Paul's Episcopal Church was organized Nov. 20, 1824, and at this time consisted of three hundred members. They occupied a brick building immediately north of the Presbyterian session room, situated on the present site of Throop's bookstore.

The First Baptist Church was organized on the 27th of October, 1827, and, at this time, had one hundred and fifty members. There was also a colored Baptist Church — which was organized January 21, 1838 — then occupying a wooden building on the south side of Lafayette street, between Brush and Beaubien. The same Society now occupy the brick building on Croghan street.

The German Lutheran Church, on Monroe avenue, was organized in 1833, and was then occupying a wooden building on the site of the present brick one. Their membership was two hundred.

The Scotch Church, on the corner of Farmer and Bates streets, was completed in October of this year, 1844. The Society was organized early in the same year, and the number of church members was sixty-five.

ORGANIZATION OF THIS CHURCH.

It will be seen from this review, that there was then no want of Churches, or Church organizations in Detroit, and the time did not seem entirely propitious for the organization of a Congregational Church; nor was Congregationalism then a favorite form of Church polity in the West, although in Michigan it had already obtained a very respectable footing. There were about fifty Congregational Churches, with a membership of about two thousand three hundred and about thirty ministers. In 1845, including this Church, there were fifty-three Congregational Churches, forty-six of which reported a membership of two thousand one hundred and fifteen, and there were thirty-two ministers. The First Presbyterian Church was, as we have said, large in numbers, strong in wealth and influence, and there was a deep conviction among many persons that the time had fully come for the organization of another Church of a similar faith, and at different times slight efforts had been made in this direction. But to CHARLES G. HAMMOND, more than to any other one man, are we indebted for the preliminary steps that led to the organization of this Church and Society, although others rendered great and invaluable aid. He was a Congregationalist by natural inclination and by education. He was converted while yet a lad of twelve years of age, living at Smyrna, N. Y., and joined a Congregational Church in the adjoining town of West Sherburne. He was also a member of a Congregational Church in Canandaigua. He came to Detroit in December, 1834, and here joined the First Presbyterian Church, and was chosen an Elder thereof in November, 1835. He subsequently, in the spring of 1836, removed to Union City, and there joined a Congregational Church. He represented Branch County in the Legislature in 1841. I was then a member of that body, and knew him well. He then exhibited the same sterling integrity of character, clear, sound judgment, and resolute purpose, and the same power to influence others, and to execute efficiently any plan which he had deliberately formed or adopted, and which, in the construction and management of the Chicago, Burlington & Quincy Railroad, placed him among the first railroad men in the land, and which has finally made him chief executive officer of the Union Pacific Railroad. In 1842, he was appointed Auditor General of the State, and the duties of his office again brought him to Detroit. He attended the Presbyterian Church, but retained his connection with the Congregational Church at Union City. He had become fully convinced that the time had come when the interests of our common faith demanded the organization of a new Church in Detroit. He saw that the city was just starting upon a new career of growth and prosperity. The Presbyterian Church was then sufficiently large to spare a portion of its strength without injury to its usefulness.

In June, 1844, his brother, the Rev. HENRY L. HAMMOND, was preaching at Homer, in this State. He studied theology at Andover; was licensed to preach in April, 1841; was ordained in December of the same year, and came to Homer, in this State, in 1842, having previously spent a year in charge of the Congregational Church at

Kingston, Mass. In June of this year, 1844, at the suggestion of his brother, he visited Detroit, to see whether it was wise to make any movement for the organization of a Congregational Church, and spent a week or two in the city. He preached once for Dr. DUFFIELD, and one Sabbath in the City Hall, and conferred with Dr. DUFFIELD upon the subject of his mission. Dr. DUFFIELD was, in conviction and feeling, a decided Presbyterian, and he had not then reached that state of catholicity of feeling which so marked his riper years. He had little confidence in Congregationalism in the abstract, still less in its adaptation to the West, and he partook of a feeling, then generally prevalent, that Western Congregationalists were not as orthodox as their New England brethren. It was ascertained that, while he admitted that there was need of a new Church, yet he was decidedly opposed to the organization of one unless it came under the care of the Presbytery, either as a Presbyterian Church, or as a Congregational Church upon the Union plan. He was then in the full vigor of his great powers, and his influence, both in the city and in the State, was very great. This opposition, for the time, discouraged further effort, and Mr. HAMMOND returned to his work at Homer. Subsequently, and probably in August, or early in September, Mr. C. G. HAMMOND, with the persistency of purpose which so marked his character, wrote to Rev. O. C. THOMPSON, then preaching at St. Clair, and one of the most prominent, most prudent and most influential of the Congregational ministers in the State. to visit Detroit and confer with Dr. DUFFIELD and other persons as to the proposed effort. Mr. THOMPSON came and called upon Dr. DUFFIELD, who listened attentively and respectfully to his representations, invited him to preach in his pulpit, and referred him to his Session. Mr. THOMPSON then saw individually most of the members of the Session, and ultimately had a meeting of a portion of them over MCFARREN'S bookstore, in SMART'S block. Among the Elders of the Presbyterian Church at that time, were some of the strongest men in the city; such men as ROBERT STUART, Major KEARSLEY, E. P. HASTINGS, Major LARNED, EDWARD BINGHAM, and HORACE HALLOCK. Several of these were present at this meeting, and especially Messrs. STUART, KEARSLEY and HASTINGS. It was at first doubtful whether this body would not throw the full weight of its power against the new enterprise, but the influence of ROBERT STUART, a man of strong and decided character, turned the scale in its favor, and it was to be countenanced rather than opposed; — and this upon the ground that it might do good to the common cause, although the chances of success were deemed very feeble. Mr. THOMPSON spent a week here in diligent endeavors to get persons enlisted, who were Congregational in sentiment, and one who thus became enlisted, had been an old parishioner at St. Clair, and has since done more to sustain the Church than any one ever connected with it—I mean Deacon SHERMAN S. BARNARD. Either at this time, or soon after, ISRAEL COE also became enlisted in the enterprise, and was one of the most important men connected with the new organization. He was a Connecticut Congregationalist, —an efficient and successful business man—of great energy and liberality.

These labors of Mr. THOMPSON were entirely gratuitous, but Mr. C. G. HAMMOND paid his fare on the boat to and from St. Clair, amounting to three dollars, and this was the first distinctive cash payment for the new Church, and was but the commencement of many such, made by the same hand, which passed into no account. Nor did the labors of Mr. THOMPSON end here. On his way to the General Association, which met at Marshall on the 24th of September of that year, he went out of his way to see the Rev. Mr. HAMMOND, at Homer, and urged him to come to Detroit, and devote himself to the organization of a Church. This visit was self-moved, and sprang entirely from the deep interest Mr. THOMPSON took in the matter, and his conviction that, under all the circumstances, Mr. HAMMOND was the best man attainable to commence and carry on the effort to successful completion, and the result proved the correctness of his judgment. Mr. HAMMOND accompanied Mr. THOMPSON to the General Association, where, doubtless, the subject was discussed by the ministers present, and in October Mr. HAMMOND came here and commenced those labors, from which this Church has sprung into existence. But, previous to the commencement of his labors, Mr. HAMMOND had been in correspondence with that eminent Christian philanthropist, DAVID HALE, of *The New York Journal of Commerce,* and had inquired of him if there was any missionary society that could render aid to the enterprise, the rules of the Home Missionary Society, at that time, restraining it from rendering aid to a new church at any place where there was already either a Presbyterian or a Congregational Church. Mr. HALE replied that *he* was, to some extent, such a society, and that, if Mr. HAMMOND and his brother thought the time had come for the effort, and he would go to Detroit and devote himself to it, he might draw upon him, Mr. HALE, for six hundred dollars per annum; and this amount was actually paid for two years, and without this, the success of the project would have been doubtful. The first services were held in the City Hall, then for a Sabbath or two in the new Scotch church, then just finished, and before they had a minister of their own. An effort was made to secure the use of the Presbyterian session room for the winter, and was well nigh successful with the trustees, but, notwithstanding what had passed between Mr. THOMPSON and the Session, it was found that the influence of the latter, as well as that of Dr. DUFFIELD, was decidedly hostile to the enterprise, and the use of the lecture room was denied. Equally hostile was the great social power of the old Society, and when the friends of the effort were driven back for the winter to the old City Hall, as the only place to be had, the prospect before them was not a cheering one. But there was no thought of discouragement. They were few in number, and not strong in wealth or social influence, but they *were* strong in earnest *purpose* and in abiding *faith*, and went forward with an unfaltering step. The leading men, at first engaged in the enterprise, were C. G. HAMMOND, ISRAEL COE, SAMUEL COIT, S. S. BARNARD, REUBEN TOWN, FRANCIS RAYMOND, LYMAN BALDWIN, E. K. GILBERT, CHARLES HOWARD, and PHILETUS S. CHURCH. Many of these were New Englanders, and were imbued with something of the true Puritan spirit.

The first meeting, of which there is any record, was at the house of CHARLES G. HAMMOND, on the 25th of November, when preliminary steps were taken to organize a Society. MARTIN WILLSON, now of Kalamazoo, was in the chair, and a committee, consisting of Messrs HAMMOND, BARNARD, BALDWIN and RAYMOND, were appointed to prepare a plan for the organization of a Society under the statute. On the 7th of December following, a notice for the meeting was given for that purpose, to be held on the 23rd of December; and on that day the Society was organized. The first meeting with reference to organizing the *Church* was, as I have mentioned, on the 8th of December. A Council was called to meet upon the 25th of the same month, and consisted of the following persons: Rev. HARVEY HYDE from Rochester, Michigan, and R. B. NEWBERRY, delegate; Rev. O. C. THOMPSON of St. Clair, and OVID SMITH, delegate; and Rev. S. A. BENTON of Armada. Mr. THOMPSON was Moderator, and Mr. BENTON, Scribe. Mr. C. G. HAMMOND presented the Articles of Faith, and, after statements from Deacon BARNARD and Rev. Mr. HAMMOND as to the reasons for organizing the Church, it was voted that the reasons were satisfactory and that a Church *be* organized. It *was* organized upon the same day, and consisted of thirteen members, namely: LYMAN BALDWIN, NANCY BALDWIN, JAMES G. CRANE, MARY A. CRANE, FRANCIS RAYMOND, RUTH RAYMOND, ROBERT W. WARNER, C. A. WARNER, WILLIAM COOK, MARIETTA P. COOK, S. S. BARNARD, MARY JANE HAMMOND, and Miss RHODA COWLES. Others had expected to join, but did not receive their letters in season. Of the thirteen that thus formed the nucleus around which this Church has crystalized, seven are still with us, namely: Mr. and Mrs. BALDWIN, Mr. and Mrs. RAYMOND, Mrs. COOK, Mr. BARNARD, and Miss COWLES; and three of them are officers in the church, namely: Deacons BARNARD, BALDWIN and RAYMOND. Nine others joined on the following Sunday, Dec. 29th, and four others on January 5th, 1845.

On that day (Jan. 5th, 1845,) it was voted to organize a Sabbath School on the following Sunday. It *was* then organized and has been kept up without intermission to the present time, and, did time permit, it would be a grateful task to recount the faithful services which have been rendered by superintendents, officers and teachers. But it must suffice to say, that the earnest labors of these Christian workers in this Sabbath School have been the means of cultivating their own growth in intellectual and Christian character, a great means of grace to the pupils, and one of the most abundant sources of increase of church membership. The only person now with us, who has, without interruption, been a member of the Sabbath School from its first organization, is FRANCIS RAYMOND. Then, too, the members of this Church have done their fair share of work in the Mission Sabbath Schools of this city, and have reaped the benefit which must ever come from such work.

One of the first steps that demanded attention was the election of Deacons, and it was voted that the afternoon of the first Sabbath of February be spent in church meeting to seek Divine guidance in the matter, and it was so spent, but no Deacons were elected until the 24th of August following, when Messrs BARNARD and HOWARD were elected Deacons for two years. On the 2d of February, 1845, FRANCIS RAYMOND was elected Clerk of the Church, as he previously had been of the Society, and he has been Clerk of both bodies from that day to this, and every word of the records of both bodies is in his handwriting, as, previous to his election, the minutes were kept merely upon slips of paper, and were by him transcribed.

ERECTION OF THE FIRST CHURCH EDIFICE.

The Church and Society had hardly come into

existence before they began to consider the great question of building a church. As early as the 31st of March, 1845, the Society authorized the purchase of the lot where the church was afterwards built, on the corner of Jefferson Avenue and Beaubien Street, at the price of two thousand dollars, and a Committee on Plans and Estimates was appointed. On the 2d of June following, a plan of building was adopted, and it was voted that the walls, roof, steeple, and, if possible, the basement, were to be built for the sum of four thousand dollars. The building was pushed with vigor, and on the 15th of December, 1845, the Society held its annual meeting in the basement, and the Church commenced worship there. They had occupied the City Hall during the winter, and after the adjournment of the Legislature, they obtained the use of the Capitol until the present Circuit Court room was completed, when, for a time, they worshiped there. As we may imagine, there was great rejoicing when they were able to meet in their own house. On the first Sabbath, Mr. HAMMOND very appropriately selected for his text the following words: "I was glad when they said unto me, Let us go into the house of the Lord."

On the 4th of January, 1846, the Committee on Building were authorized to increase the debt so that the interest thereon should not exceed two hundred dollars per annum; on the 10th of March, 1846, the plan for the interior of the church was adopted; on the 14th of March a contract for its completion was authorized; and on the 30th of August following the completed church edifice was dedicated to the worship of God. The cost of the lot was two thousand dollars, and the house cost over five thousand dollars, while a subscription of about four thousand one hundred and ninety dollars had been obtained. This included an Eastern subscription, obtained by Rev. Mr. HAMMOND, of nine hundred and seventy-three dollars and twenty cents. There remained upon the lot and building a debt of not far from three thousand dollars. The leading subscribers belonging to the Church and Society were ISRAEL COE, CHARLES G. HAMMOND, SAMUEL COIT, REUBEN TOWN, S. S. BARNARD, FRANCIS RAYMOND, LYMAN BALDWIN, and H. T. BACKUS. Quite liberal subscriptions, however, were received from those who belonged neither to Church nor Society. BUCKMINSTER WIGHT subscribed one hundred dollars, WESLEY TRUESDAIL fifty dollars, and others smaller sums. We may well believe that this subscription, small as it was, was an exhibition upon the part of the Church and Society, of great liberality, and the occasion of no little self-sacrifice.

MR. HAMMOND AND HIS LABORS.

For the first year, the salary of Mr. HAMMOND had mainly been paid by the contribution of Mr. HALE. His contribution for the second year formed a part of the Eastern subscription for the church, and Mr. HAMMOND'S salary, or a portion thereof, was paid by the Connecticut Missionary Society. On the 9th of November, 1846, the Trustees were authorized to employ Mr. HAMMOND for a year, at a salary of seven hundred dollars, and this arrangement was completed. During the following winter, the Rev. CHARLES G. FINNEY labored here for some six weeks in connection with the Pastor, and it resulted in a very interesting work of grace, and quite a number were added to the Church, and a deeper interest in the subject of religion was awakened throughout the city.

On the 21st of June, 1847, Mr. HAMMOND asked to be released from his engagement for the year after the 30th of June. The Society requested him to engage for another year, but he declined, and the Church and Society then, by vote, expressed their confidence in him and their commendation of his ministerial labors. On the 5th of July, 1847, Mr. HAMMOND administered the communion, and this closed his regular services with the Church. The period of the ministry of Mr. HAMMOND was both the formative and the critical period of the history of our Church. It had struggled with poverty, embarrassment, obscurity, and, to some extent, with contemptuous neglect. Through it all, the labors of Mr. HAMMOND were faithful, wise, and tireless, and received the blessing of the Heavenly Father. Special efforts were made to interest those who were Congregational in sentiment, and those who attended no church. He devoted much time to visiting and other personal efforts, and never lost sight of the great end of Christian work—the conversion of the soul to God. The prayer-meetings were spirited and spiritual. The whole number added to the Church during his ministry, including the original thirteen, was one hundred and fifteen, of which one hundred and ten remained at his departure. A comfortable, though not elegant, edifice had been erected and completed. The congregation had largely increased, and it had become entirely respectable to belong to the Church and Society, and the Church had obtained recognition among the sisterhood of churches, and its influence in awakening others to more active Christian work and to higher spiritual life was apparent. The labors of Mr. HAMMOND are held in the highest estimation by those who then belonged to the Church and Society.

Mr. HAMMOND was immediately succeeded by

Rev. O. C. THOMPSON, who had been compelled to leave his parish at St. Clair because of ill-health. He preached for about two months, when his health failed and he was compelled, to the deep regret of the Church and Society, to suspend his ministerial labors, which he did for many years. The Rev. Mr. KELLOGG thereafter, for a short time, filled the pulpit, and, on the 11th of November, 1847, the Trustees were authorized to employ Rev. W. W. ATTERBURY for six months, at a salary of two hundred and fifty dollars. Mr. ATTERBURY was a young man, just out of the seminary, but he proved an acceptable and faithful minister. During the winter of 1847–48, the Rev. Mr. AVERY labored in the Church, as an Evangelist, in connection with Mr. ATTERBURY, and these labors were attended with deep interest.

DR. KITCHEL'S MINISTRY.

On the 10th of July, 1848, the Church and Society, with great unanimity, called to the pastorate Rev. H. D. KITCHEL, then of Thomaston, Conn., at a salary of one thousand dollars. Mr. KITCHEL graduated at Middlebury in 1835; studied theology one year at Andover, then, while acting as tutor at Middlebury, studied another year with Dr. MERRILL, (a man of pre-eminent ability, who took the valedictory at Dartmouth, in a class of which DANIEL WEBSTER was a member) and graduated at the Theological Seminary, at New Haven, in 1838. In the fall of the same year, he commenced preaching at Thomaston, and was ordained Pastor in February, 1839. He remained at that place until he came to Detroit. He was obtained as Pastor of this Church through the agency and recommendation of Mr. COE, a Connecticut man, who well knew the wants of the Church, and the qualifications necessary to supply them. Mr. KITCHEL accepted the call, preached his first sermon on the 1st of October, and on the 6th of December following was installed as Pastor of the Church. Rev. Dr. DUFFIELD was a member of the Council of Installation — conducted the examination (a most satisfactory one) — and took part in the installation exercises.

Mr. KITCHEL remained the Pastor of the Church until dismissed by a Council, at his own request, on the 2d of November, 1864, a term of sixteen years. The period of his ministry was one of prosperity and growth, and, like times of peace to the national historian, affords but few points of special interest to the historical narrator. The new Pastor was soon recognized as one of the most cultivated and able ministers, not only of the city, but of the State and of the West. His sermons were characterized by soundness of doctrine, fullness and ripeness of thought, with a purity of style, and chasteness of diction that gave them a great charm, and made them a power for good. They were eminently suggestive in their character, and were especially attractive to the thoughtful. The effect was a gradual and rapid increase in the Church and Society, so that, in four years' time, the building so recently erected was filled to overflowing, and no seats were to be had, and a fair proportion of these accessions were persons of culture and social position. This forced upon the Society the question of the erection of a new church; and this forms an important chapter in our history, not without its disagreeable incidents, and if for no other purpose than to warn others of the shoal on which we were so nearly stranded, it is worthy of record.

ERECTION OF THE SECOND CHURCH EDIFICE.

The first formal meeting with reference to a new church edifice, was on the 21st of December, 1852, a little over six years from the time the first church was completed. Three projects were considered: *first,* the erection of a new central edifice; *second,* enlarging the old one; *third,* colonizing and organizing a *new* Church. A committee consisting of Messrs. HOLMES, BARNARD, O. C. THOMPSON, WALKER, PARSONS, and S. G. WIGHT, were appointed to consider the several projects, and report at an adjourned meeting the following week. On the 28th of December, the committee reported in favor of the erection of a new edifice in a central part of the town, and time was given to them to report as to the proper location. On the 10th of January, 1853, the Society voted to proceed with the erection of a new church. The committee reported in favor of a site on the corner of Monroe avenue and Farmer street, but the subject was recommitted to them, and they were instructed to inquire as to obtaining the lot on the corner of Congress and Griswold streets, where Buhl's Bank Block now stands; but, on the 21st of February, they reported in favor of purchasing the present site at a cost of ten thousand dollars. A Committee on Subscriptions was appointed, consisting of Messrs. BUTLER, STEBBINS, BARNARD, and PARSONS; and a Committee on Plans, consisting of Messrs. H. D. A. WARD, COE, S. M. HOLMES, and WALKER. On the 6th of March, the Committee on Subscriptions reported that they had obtained subscriptions to the amount of eleven thousand six hundred and sixty-four dollars. The Committee on Plans reported a plan, and they were instructed so to modify it, that the cost of the new church should not exceed twenty thousand dollars. A Building Committee was appointed, consisting of Messrs. HOLMES, BARNARD, GILBERT, PARSONS, BUTLER, and KING, and the Trustees, and that committee were authorized to offer the old church edifice for sale, possession to be given the following December. By the 27th of June, it was ascertained that the cost of the building, according to the plan adopted, would far exceed twenty thousand dollars and the committee were authorized to enlarge the cost, but to limit it as near thirty thousand dollars as the plan would admit of. This virtually left the Building Committee with unlimited power to build according, to the plan, whatever it cost. Although the Society was not rich, and its resources were very limited, yet the prospects before it seemed bright and hopeful. We had a popular minister, a growing Church and Society, and we looked forward to a large increase of both. We were ambitious to have a church of which we could be proud, and that would be an ornament to the city. Business generally was prosperous, and business men were full of hopeful courage. The leading men on the Building Committee, and upon whom the great burden fell, Messrs. HOLMES and BARNARD, were men of means, of earnest zeal and large-hearted liberality, and they freely advanced their means and credit to meet the exigency of the occasion. Fortunately, or unfortunately, we were not compelled to pay anything down upon the lot—indeed, owing to a controversy upon the amount due upon a mortgage thereon, we were not at liberty to pay anything until that controversy was settled. The result was that this edifice was completed at a cost, exclusive of the lot, of forty-five thousand nine hundred and eight dollars, and sixteen cents. It is but just to say, however, that nearly twelve thousand dollars of this was not included in the estimate of the expenses of the building, namely: the cost of gas-fitting and fixtures, upholstering and furnishing, the bell, the organ, the furniture for the house, fence, etc., etc. Our resources applicable to meet this large cost were as follows:

Sale of old building on the lot,	$436 00
Collected by ladies to pay for bell,	974 74
Sale of old church,	9,150 00
Received on subscriptions,	11,205 75
Sale of pews on completion of church,	6,628 50
Total resources,	$28,394 99

Leaving unprovided for towards the house alone, seventeen thousand five hundred and thirteen dollars and fourteen cents, besides the cost of the lot, ten thousand dollars, and its accruing interest.

The house was dedicated with appropriate services on the 21st of September, 1854. After paying the subscriptions for building the house and the money for the purchase of pews, the Society were unable to make any present effort to reduce this large debt. Our income from pew rents did not pay our current expenses, but our creditors were forbearing, and we rested, hoping for the time soon to come when we could make an energetic effort to reduce, if not pay, the indebtedness. While looking for this good time coming, there came upon us, as a thunder storm from a clear sky, the financial crash of the autumn of 1857, which most seriously affected the pecuniary ability of some of our best men and cast a deep gloom over business prospects.

The annual meeting held on the 21st of December, 1857, was one of deep gloom. Our indebtedness at that time, including the accruing interest, was thirty-seven thousand and sixty-two dollars, besides a paving tax, unprovided for, of nearly a thousand dollars. In round numbers we owed thirty-eight thousand dollars, and were utterly destitute of resources. We hardly dared to speak of the dangers that loomed up before us, but they were deeply felt by thoughtful men. Various plans for reducing this debt were discussed from time to time, and efforts made, but nothing practical was done until December, 1859, when, by an earnest and self-denying effort upon the part of the Society, met by a spirit of exceeding liberality on the part of our creditors, our floating debt was paid, leaving unpaid the purchase price of the lot and its interest, and the claim for paving taxes. While the subscription made taxed the liberality and the means of the Society, it would have failed in accomplishing the object except for the large-hearted generosity of our principal creditor, Deacon BARNARD, who received a large portion of the indebtedness in unsold pews from which he could derive no income save as they were rented beyond the assessments thereon for society purposes. There still remained upon us, however, a heavy indebtedness, and the efforts so far made, encouraged us to make provision for the payment of that. In making arrangement for the paying off of the first installment of our debt and providing for the remainder, we were largely indebted to the sound judgment and great financial ability of one who is no longer with us, WILLIAM WARNER, but he will be spoken of elsewhere, and by another. Arrangements were made for taking up collections on the Sabbath towards the reduction of our debt, and in 1863, it was found we could pay off our debt upon the lot for fourteen thousand dollars. The unpaid taxes were a thousand dollars, and our church imperatively needed repairs to the amount of another thousand, thus leaving sixteen thousand dollars to be provided for. A second great effort was made to meet these obligations, and this effort was successful. We had raised by our Sunday collections more than two thousand dollars, and the balance of the sum required was raised by subscription. In both these instances, the subscriptions were most cheerfully met, and nearly every member of the Church and Society joined in the effort. The experience was a bitter one, and, although it has not been without its good results in teaching us self-sacrifice and how to bear burdens, I would advise no Society to follow our example. It unquestionably seriously interfered with our prosperity, for persons coming into the city did not desire to join a Church or a Society where they must bear the burden of an old debt.

During the building of the church, and in December, 1854, the society voted six months' leave of absence to Dr. KITCHEL, with the continuance of his salary, and he availed himself of this absence to visit Europe and the Holy Land. A liberal contribution towards his expenses was also made by individual members of the Church and Society.

I have already said that the church was dedicated on the 21st of September, 1854. It is proper to say that the Rev. Dr. LEONARD BACON was appropriately selected to preach the dedicatory sermon. He was a native of Detroit, the son of a Congregational minister who resided here for a time and who was, doubtless, the first Congregational minister that ever preached in the city.

MRS. KITCHEL.

On the 1st day of June, 1858, the Church and Society met with a most grievous loss in the death of Mrs. ANNA S. KITCHEL, the wife of our Pastor. Hers was a character of rare excellence. She breathed the very spirit of piety almost from her childhood. With great native strength and force, as well as tenderness of character, cultivated by education, refined by social intercourse, and purified and elevated by a deep and earnest piety, she united a retiring, almost shrinking, modesty, and an entire absence of self-assertion, that prevented those who knew her but slightly from fully appreciating her great worth and real power. What she was in the sacred circle of home and to those allied to her by the tenderest ties known to our humanity, of daughter, wife, and mother, I cannot fully know, and if I did, this would not be the fitting occasion for utterance. I speak of her only as our Pastor's wife, and a member of this Church. As such, her labors were at once unobtrusive and untiring. If any member of the Church or congregation was in distress of mind, body, or estate, she seemed to know it by intuition, and to be present with her words of counsel, comfort and sympathy, and with her deeds of charity, kindness and love. But she did not rest contented with her own personal exertion. As occasion demanded, she called freely upon others to do what she could not do herself, and she had the rare power, without officiousness, of knowing what others could and ought to do, and setting them to work. Many in this audience can bear witness to the reception of her ever discreet and kindly notes of suggestion, breathing the very spirit of the Master; and her touching invitations to come to the Savior were a power for good that wonderfully complemented the labors of the pulpit. She often gathered about her at her own home the young of the Church and Society, and while she promoted, in her gentle way, every social enjoyment, she never for a moment lost sight of their spiritual interest. The spirit of her daily life was in perfect harmony with her Christian labors. Her loss to the Church was *irreparable*. It came so suddenly, that, while it stunned and almost paralyzed us, we did not at the time so fully appreciate it as we did afterward—as month after month passed away and the want of her presence and influence was more and more understood and felt.

Many years after, in 1864, we were called upon to mourn the death of the second Mrs. KITCHEL. She came amongst us a stranger from a distant State where her church connections were, and she remained with us so short a time, and was so much of an invalid while with us, that she did not become a part of our Society as did the first Mrs. KITCHEL. Those who knew her well speak of her in the highest terms of commendation as an accomplished, earnest, and religious woman. Her loss fell sadly and heavily upon our Pastor, and called forth the deep and earnest sympathy of the Church and congregation.

CLOSE OF DR. KITCHEL'S PASTORATE.

On the 21st of October, 1864, Dr. KITCHEL asked a dismission from the Church with reference to accepting a call from Chicago, and on the 2d of November, a Council met and acquiesced in his request; and thus was completed the sixteenth year of his pastorship of this Church. During that time the Church had largely increased in numbers, strength and influence. There had been added by letter, one hundred and eighteen males, and two hundred and thirty-one females; by profession of faith, sixty-one males and one hundred and twenty-two females—in all, five hundred and thirty-two. Many of these were gathered in during the time of the great revival of 1857–8.

MR. FREELAND'S MINISTRY.

On the 2d of December, 1864, the Rev. S. M.

FREELAND, who had been preaching at Watertown, Conn., was engaged for three months. He came at a very interesting time, when there was considerable religious interest in the city. That interest was increased and deepened, and our own Church shared in the fruits of the revival. His labors were so acceptable that, on the 20th of March, 1865, he was engaged for a year. Before that year expired, the project of organizing a second Congregational Church was freely discussed, both amongst individuals and in our Church gatherings. Many of those who had borne the great burden of the past indebtedness upon their shoulders were anxious for something of rest, and were desirous, for a time, at least, of having a large Church from which the expense of supporting the gospel could be readily raised, while some had doubts whether the time had fully come for the organization of such a Church. But, after full discussion, on the 6th of March, 1866, it was voted that it was expedient to organize a second Congregational Church, and this Church was subsequently organized and Mr. FREELAND became its Pastor. The number dismissed from our Church to organize this was one hundred and ten. Thus this Church somewhat reluctantly became a Mother Church, and, in so doing, lost many of its most valuable Christian workers, but she has reason fully to be satisfied with the result. The Daughter Church is one of which she may be gratefully proud, and already nearly rivals in numbers and in strength the Mother from which she sprang. God's rich blessings have attended the movement.

DR. BALLARD CALLED.

In April, 1866, the Rev. Mr. BALLARD, of Williamstown, Mass., supplied our pulpit for three Sabbaths, and so acceptable were his labors that, on the 6th of May, a call was extended to him to become our Pastor. This call was accepted and he commenced his labors in June following, and was regularly installed Pastor of the Church on the 18th of October, 1866. There have been added to the Church during his ministry sixty-six members. His labors have been eminently acceptable and the Church are very thoroughly united in his support.

I cannot forbear mentioning here one event of a personal character. On the 21st of December, 1868, Deacon BARNARD resigned his position as Trustee of this Church, after seventeen years of most faithful and arduous service. He had been emphatically the working man of the Board, and the indebtedness of the Society to him in this, as well as in other particulars, is very great.

The whole number admitted to the Church membership since the organization has been eight hundred and forty-five. Some of these have gone from us, because they were not of us; many have gone over the River, and are awaiting us in the Better Land; still a larger number are widely scattered over our country, members of other Churches; and two hundred and seventy-five still remain upon our list. But the influence of this Church for good, has not, we trust, been limited to church membership.

SALARIES.

I have already mentioned that, on the 9th of November, 1846, Mr. HAMMOND was voted a salary of seven hundred dollars. In 1848, Mr. KITCHEL was settled at a salary of one thousand dollars. On the 21st of December, 1852, this was raised to twelve hundred dollars; in December, 1855, to sixteen hundred; on the 1st of May, 1857, to two thousand dollars. On the 21st of March, 1865, the salary of Mr. FREELAND was fixed at twenty-five hundred dollars; and Mr. BALLARD was settled as Pastor at that salary. From the 1st of February, 1868, his salary has been three thousand dollars. This shows that the Church and Society, even in the midst of embarrassments, have been progressive in this matter of salaries, and have not fallen behind other societies even of much greater wealth.

WOMEN'S VOTING.

The question of the age, the right of women to vote, yet remains unsettled in this Church. On the 9th of February, 1845, it was moved that female members be permitted to vote on the admission of members. This was laid upon the table under the rule, and, for aught that appears upon the records, it still lies there. In March, 1861, women were permitted to vote on the election of Deacons. On the 6th of May, 1866, when the question was before the church as to extending a call to the Rev. Dr. Ballard, it was moved that female members be permitted to vote. This motion was also laid upon the table. These motions are not *buried,* they only *sleep,* and they have laid upon this imaginary table of the Clerk's record about as long as they will be quiet, and we may as well prepare to give them a fair hearing.

TERM OF THE DIACONATE.

The question whether Deacons should be elected for a limited time, or whether the office should be a permanent one, is also somewhat of an open question in this Church, and I give the action of the Church upon the subject. On the 25th of August, 1845, Deacons BARNARD and HOWARD were elected the first Deacons for the term of two years. On the 23d of December, 1847, they were re-elected. On the 23d of November, 1849, it was voted to elect three Deacons, whose term of office should expire on the 1st of January, 1852, and Deacons BARNARD and HOWARD were re-elected, and S. M. HOLMES added to the list. In 1852, on the 9th of January, these three were re-elected, and on the 18th of January, 1856, Deacons RAYMOND and BALDWIN were added to the list. In 1861, January 22d, Mr. HOLMES having resigned, and Mr. HOWARD having removed, there was a new election at which women voted, and brothers BARNARD, RAYMOND, WALKER and WARNER were elected. On the 27th of January, 1865, all resigned, when, on the motion of brother WARNER, Deacons were elected, subject to Congregational usage, and brothers BARNARD, BALDWIN, RAYMOND and PARTRIDGE were elected. On the 18th of January, 1866, brothers WALKER and SILSBEE were added to the list. On the 21st of October, 1868, brother PARTRIDGE having removed and brother SILSBEE having joined the Second Congregational Church, brothers BAKER and BOSTWICK were elected. The question has been more than once discussed whether the office should be a permanent one, or for a limited time, and a committee was appointed by the Church, consisting of brethren entertaining diverse views, to examine the question and report upon that subject, but that committee have failed to report, and the question is still an open one; and whether the present Deacons hold their office at the will of the Church, or for life, depends upon what is Congregational usage.

BENEFACTIONS OF THE CHURCH.

While the Church has been deficient in many things, and doubtless deficient in the highest spirit of Christian labor, yet, during all the pecuniary embarrassments that have weighed upon us, the Church has contributed freely and largely to the various benevolent causes that have demanded Christian aid, and I think the statistics, which, however, cannot be readily gathered and compared, would show that, in this respect, we have exceeded the liberality of most Churches of the same wealth and financial ability.

POSITION ON THE TEMPERANCE QUESTION.

The Church, too, has borne an earnest testimony in favor of the cause of Temperance. As early as March 28, 1849, the Church approved of the Temperance League, then formed in the city, and a committee was appointed to represent this Church on the Executive Committee, consisting of Messrs. HAMMOND, HOLMES, and the Pastor. On the 21st of December, 1849, a resolution, drawn by Dr. KITCHEL, was adopted by the Church, and still stands upon its records; and, consistent with this resolution, has been the spirit and action of the Church from that time to the present. This resolution is in the following words:

"Deeply impressed with the prevalence of intemperance in the community around us, and with the conviction that the inconsiderate and moderate use of intoxicating drinks is the fountain-head of this evil; believing also that a special responsibility rests on the Churches of CHRIST, that they carefully maintain their own purity in this respect, and throw around them the influence of a blameless example, this Church, for the purpose of an Act and Testimony to the world, and to secure to itself and to the cause of CHRIST, as far as may be practicable, the moral power of a right profession and unsullied membership, declares its full conviction that the manufacture, sale, or use of intoxicating drinks as a beverage is at variance with the spirit and teachings of CHRIST and His Holy Word, and should be, on grounds of Christian obligation, altogether abandoned and discouraged by all who bear the Christian name. And to this end, besides our other modes of action against this evil, a book shall be kept by the Clerk of this Church, containing this our Declaration, which shall be presented for signature to every person desiring connection with this Church — not as a condition of their acceptance, nor as a sole test of character, but with the most earnest desire that our entire membership may stand unitedly and fully arrayed against this great evil.

"We, therefore, whose names follow, members of the First Congregational Church of Detroit, do covenant together that we will not make, sell, or use intoxicating drinks as a beverage, and that we, in all fit methods, will discountenance the same in others."

CONTRIBUTIONS TO THE WAR OF THE REBELLION.

There is one chapter in the history of our Church and Society that cannot be overlooked on an occasion like this, and yet which can only be adverted to, although the materials in my hands tempt me to a history that would be full of graphic interest — that is, the aid rendered our common country during the recent war for our national existence. While, upon minor topics of modes and measures, there was naturally some difference of opinion, there was none as to the atrocity of the Rebellion, and the stern duty of crushing it out by the strong arm and power of the Government. This deep and earnest feeling found voice again and again in the pulpit, and was evinced by the self-sacrificing spirit of liberality that led to large and frequent contributions to all the purposes of the war; but of these I cannot speak, although some of them deserve special commendation. I can only mention those who gave personal services directly to their country.

At the commencement of the rebellion, JOHN TYLER enlisted as a private in Company A, of the 1st Regiment of Michigan Infantry Volunteers, called for three months' service, and commanded by Colonel O. B. Wilcox. Private TYLER was engaged in the first battle of Bull Run, and served until the expiration of his term of service. In July, 1862, he joined the 17th Regiment of Michigan Infantry as First Lieutenant, was engaged at the battles of South Mountain, Antietam, and Fredericksburg, was commissioned as Captain in June, 1863; was with his regiment at the siege of Vicksburg, and in several battles incident thereto. At the battle of Campbell's Station, in East Tennessee, he was twice wounded, and lost his left hand, and was subsequently brevetted as Major of Volunteers for gallant conduct in that battle. In May, 1864, he was appointed Captain in the 2d Regiment of the Veteran Reserve Corps; and since the war has been commissioned as First Lieutenant in the 43d Regiment of United States Infantry, in which he is now serving.

Next upon the list, in point of time, was FRANK R. RICE, who enlisted for three months in the 1st Michigan Infantry, at the very breaking out of the war, May 1, 1861. He re-enlisted on the 1st of September, as Sergeant, and won his way by genuine valor to a Second Lieutenantcy, and to a First Lieutenantcy on the 1st of November following. At the battle of Fredericksburg, December 13, 1862, he lost his leg and was subsequently transferred to the Veteran Reserve Corps, as First Lieutenant, and has since been transferred to the 44th U. S. Infantry, to which he now belongs.

HENRY W. NALL became First Lieutenant of the

7th Michigan Infantry in July, 1861, and was then promoted to the Captaincy, and on the organization of the 24th Michigan Infantry, was selected as Major of that popular regiment. He was engaged in many skirmishes and battles, and acquitted himself like a true soldier. The last battle in which he was engaged was that of Fredericksburg, December 13, 1862. He was subsequently sent home on a furlough, from failing health, and died from disease contracted in the service on the 3d of July, 1863.

CHARLES J. NALL enlisted, after the defeat of Bull Run, in the regular army, as a private, was promoted to the medical staff December 1st of the same year; was in nine general engagements, and was most honorably discharged, after arduous service, for ill-health, July 26, 1864.

FRANCIS RAYMOND, Jr., enlisted on the same day, July 24, 1861, as a private in the 24th Regiment; became Sergeant, August 19, and Commissary Sergeant April 5, 1863, First Lieutenant and Adjutant, April 26, 1864; received his commission as Captain July 15, 1866; was wounded at the battle of the Wilderness, May 5, 1864, and honorably discharged July 9, 1865.

EDWIN S. ACKER enlisted August 15, 1861, as Sergeant in the 9th Michigan Infantry; was wounded at the battle of Tullahoma, June 13, 1862, and received a commission as First Lieutenant in the regular army, March 16, 1863.

JAMES C. ACKER, his brother, enlisted as Sergeant in the 2d Michigan Cavalry, August 31, 1861; was clerk to General Sheridan when he commanded that Regiment; was promoted to Acting Adjutant, awaiting commission as First Lieutenant, but was taken prisoner in one of Morgan's raids; was subsequently paroled, and afterwards exchanged, and then became clerk of the military prison at Louisville, Ky., and served his full three years.

CHARLES H. CURTIS enlisted August 22, 1861, as Quarter-Master Sergeant in the 7th Michigan Infantry; was commissioned Second Lieutenant, April 15, 1862, First Lieutenant, February 10, 1863, and Captain May 2, 1864. He participated in all the campaigns of the Army of the Potomac, including the seven days of battle before Richmond under McClellan, the battle of Gettysburg, and the long struggle so familiar to all, till the army of Grant was in front of Petersburg. On the 17th of June, 1864, owing to severe and protracted ill-health, he was compelled to resign, after nearly three years of most active and gallant service.

STEPHEN S. BARROWS went into the service October 12, 1861, as Second Lieutenant in the 9th Michigan Infantry, and received his commission as First Lieutenant on the 13th day of December, 1861. He was taken prisoner at Murfreesboro, Tenn., July 13, 1862, and was released on the 16th day of the same month; was promoted to the rank of Captain, February 27, 1863, and was mustered out of the army at the expiration of his term of service, November 13, 1864.

WILLIAM S. BLISS entered the army October 13, 1861, as First Lieutenant in Battery B, of the Michigan Light Artillery; was taken prisoner at Shiloh, April 6, 1862, and foully murdered by a sentinel at Montgomery, Ala., May 1, 1862.

LAFAYETTE F. HARTER became Paymaster in the Navy, December, 1861, and served to the close of the war under Admirals Davis, Porter, and Lee, in the Mississippi squadron.

EDWIN M. CONKLIN enlisted September 3, 1861, in Company E, 9th Michigan Infantry, and during his first year of service died at Tullahoma, Tenn., July 3, 1862, of congestion of the lungs occasioned by a forced march.

GEORGE M. LANE became Captain of Company B, of the 1st Michigan Engineers, April, 1862, served under Buel and Rosecrans, was engaged in the battle of Stone River, was subsequently Adjutant General in the Provost Marshal General's department in Kentucky till the close of the war, and was mustered out as Brevet Major in April, 1866. The services of this regiment were invaluable, but mainly in the civil department as engineers.

GROVER S. WORMER entered the army as Captain in the 8th Cavalry Regiment, served during the war, was engaged in many battles under different distinguished Generals of the war, and was promoted to a Brigadier Generalship.

FREDERICK W. SWIFT became Captain of Company F, in the famous 17th Regiment, in July, 1862, and on the 11th of September joined the 9th Army Corps, and served until the close of the war. He was in command of the regiment for most of the time after September, 1863, and was taken prisoner at Spottsylvania Court House, May 4, 1864, in a battle where his regiment was terribly cut to pieces; was taken to Lynchburg, Macon, and, finally, to Charleston, and was one of the fifty Federal officers placed under fire as hostages for the safety of that city. He was exchanged August 3, rejoined his regiment in September, and served till the close of the war. He was appointed Colonel of Volunteers for gallant and meritorious conduct at Spottsylvania, and was also made a Brevet Brigadier General for gallant and meritorious conduct during the war.

HERBERT ADAMS enlisted as Sergeant of Company H, 24th Michigan Infantry, August 4, 1862, was with his regiment at the battle of Fredericksburg, was afterwards taken sick and died at Belle Plains, Va., January 4, 1863.

In the spring of 1862, after the battle of Corinth, Dr. DWIGHT STEBBINS, in response to a call for relief to aid in the care of the sick and wounded in our Michigan Regiments, volunteered his services to the Sanitary Commission, and by that efficient agency was appointed to the hospitals at Corinth. So great was the demand for his services by those who needed immediate aid and attention, and so earnest and sympathetic was his nature, that he could give himself no rest from constant, unremitting labor, while others suffered. Worn with fatigue, he was at length himself seized with camp fever. After ten days of illness, and while still prostrated by disease, and almost in a dying state, he was conveyed to a steamer bound for Cairo, but died as the boat reached the latter place, on the evening of July 18, 1862.

LUTHER S. TROWBRIDGE joined the 5th Michigan Cavalry, September, 1862. This regiment formed a part of the famous Michigan Cavalry Brigade, and its history is a part of the history of the country. They were in fourteen engagements in fifteen days at the time of Lee's raid into Pennsylvania. He was in command of the regiment at the time; and, in the fall of 1863, was made Lieutenant Colonel of the 10th

Michigan Cavalry, and Colonel in 1864; was in East Tennessee during 1864, engaged in active, arduous and efficient service; January 20, 1865, was made Provost Marshal General of East Tennessee, and joined Stoneman in his raids upon the railroads to cut off Davis' retreat in March following, and was engaged in the chase after Davis, marching two thousand miles in sixty-nine days; and at the close of the war was brevetted Brigadier General and Major General for gallant and meritorious services.

Rev. ORRIN C. THOMPSON, on the 7th of June, 1864, engaged in the service of the Christian Commission, and continued therein till October 1, 1865.

His son, ORRIN C. THOMPSON, Jr., engaged in the same service in August, 1864, and enlisted in the army, March, 1865, and continued therein till September, 1865.

His daughter, MAGGIE E. THOMPSON, was likewise engaged one year in the most efficient and valuable hospital service.

These are our representatives in the army and upon the field of battle: for such a representation we may be both grateful and proud. There are those who are now with us who served the country with equal fidelity and courage, although they were not of us when these services were rendered.

HENRY D. EDWARDS entered the 1st Massachusetts Cavalry Regiment at the commencement of the war, and was transferred to the Navy as Master's Mate in February, 1862, and served most efficiently and gallantly until August, 1865, and was promoted to Paymaster in the Navy.

PHILETUS W. NORRIS entered an Ohio regiment as private, in the spring of 1861, and the next year raised and commanded a company; was wounded, and, from poor health, compelled to leave active service, but was most efficient in promoting the good cause at home.

WILLIAM STOCKING enlisted in 1864 in the 60th Massachusetts Regiment, and rendered service as a private in the ranks.

CONCLUSION.

Such, my friends, is the sketch I have to offer you. It is meager and imperfect from the stern necessity laid upon me of rejecting an immense mass of material at my hand for a fuller history. However imperfectly recorded in these pages, our history of the past is recorded above, and that record cannot be changed. Imperfect as have been our efforts and our service, we may well hope that the Master's blessing has rested upon us.

The wide-reaching influences for good originating here, have done and are doing their proper and legitimate work, and will continue to do that work for all time. The future is yet before us ; its history has not only yet to be written, but is yet to be made ; we—you, and I, and those that come after us—are to make that history. This Church should be a living power in this city for good. We have no secret roots of bitterness in our midst, no discord ; harmony prevails among the people, and between Pastor and people. We have a good church edifice, paid for, after much tribulation, and in a central location, and a large Church membership. But these are not ends, but means—elements of a living, vital force to be used as such. We are to do our part in the great work of converting the world to God. While we forget not this work abroad, our great work is at *home;* and the order of this work is Christian *being*, Christian *living*, and Christian *doing*.

I have already stated, that, at the time when this Church was organized, Congregationalism had not a strong position in the West. Many of its ministers were graduates of Oberlin ; and, while it was admitted that they were earnest Christian workers, either with or without cause, Oberlin was not in good repute as to orthodoxy among other denominations. This Church immediately became associated with the other Congregational Churches of the State, and with them suffered from whatever prejudice existed on this subject. But that prejudice no longer exists, either against this Church or Congregational Churches at large. They have the entire confidence of other evangelical denominations, and Congregationalism to-day needs no vindication in Michigan.

There are in this State one hundred and seventy-five Congregational Churches, with an aggregate of ten thousand eight hundred and eighty-four members and one hundred and forty-five ministers; and these Churches compare favorably with the Churches of any other denomination in all the elements that make efficient, working Christian Churches, while the ministers are an intelligent, cultivated, earnest body of men, comprising a full average amount of ability of the highest order. The Church polity, too, has been found not only adapted to the West, but peculiarly fitted for the Western mind, that not only theoretically *recognizes*, but *believes* with practical earnestness in the perfect equality of men before God and the Law, and has little faith in ecclesiastical domination.

At the commencement of this address, I referred to Detroit as it was in 1844. What it is now, I need not describe. The recent census of the school children indicates a population of from eighty to one hundred thousand. It has become a great commercial and manufacturing metropolis. Its increase throws upon the Christian Churches and the Christian men and women of this city, great duties and important responsibilities. The element of religious power, so far as Churches and Church members are concerned, has increased somewhat in proportion to the growth of our city. There are forty-nine professedly Christian Churches in this city, as follows: ten Catholic Churches, two of which are German and one Colored, with a Catholic population numbering about thirty thousand five hundred, served by one Bishop and twenty-two Priests; four Presbyterian Churches, numbering ten hundred and seventy-seven members; one Scotch Church, numbering three hundred and fifty members; one United Presbyterian Church of two hundred and eighty members; six Episcopal Churches, with a membership of seventeen hundred and ninety-eight; four Methodist Episcopal Churches, with a membership of ten hundred and sixty-six and eighty-one probationers; one Protestant Methodist Church, with a small number of members; five Baptist Churches with eight hundred and four members, including one German, one French and one Colored; seven German Protestant Churches, with a membership of about two thousand; three Christian Churches, or Churches of Christ, with two hundred and ninety-five members; two Congregational Churches, with four hundred and fifty-five members; one Unitarian Church, with three hundred members; one Swedenborgian Church, with sixty members. These Churches are a power for good in our midst, and that power ought to be, and might be, almost indefinitely increased. That increase of power must, under God, depend mainly upon two things: first, the true Christian character of the professed Church members; secondly, their wisdom, earnestness and faithful efficiency in Christian work.

The masses of the people need to be brought more directly under Christian influence. We need to bring within the walls of our churches, and within the embrace of a warm Christian sympathy, the men who wear blouses and have faces begrimed with the sweat and soil of shops, and hands hardened with toil. These men need to be made to feel that, beneath the rough exterior, we recognize and appreciate their genuine manhood, their oneness with ourselves, their childhood of a common Father, and that they are most cordially welcome among us. As a class, they will not accept our condescension, nor will they meekly take the back or cheap seats in our churches, nor be gathered in mission chapels. As one element in a better state of things, I look forward with hope to the time when some other way will be devised of supporting our ministers and the expenses of our Churches than by pew rents. All seats should be alike freely open to all, and here, of all places on earth, should there be true equality, and no human soul should be driven from the house of God because he cannot, or does not desire to pay the rent of a pew, or because he is too proud to confess his poverty and take a cheap seat, or one free of rent, while others pay. Our ministers and our Church members need more fully to appreciate and sympathise with the trials and temptations of *common* men and women in *common* life, and to understand the good there is in unchristian men, and to acquire at the foot of the Cross and in the careful study of the character and history of our Savior, the power of awakening in sinful souls the aspirations slumbering there for a nobler and spiritual life. If the Churches which claim to be evangelical, and can, therefore, to some extent, work in concert, were, in the spirit of their Master. each in its own sphere, to unite to extend the power of a living Christian faith in our city, it would be difficult to fix limits to the good which could be accomplished. We cannot neglect the exercise of this power and be guiltless. As members of this Church and Society, let us not be behindhand in this work, which demands, in the name of God and our common humanity, our noblest and most earnest efforts.

ANNIVERSARY POEM,

BY

MRS. JULIA P. BALLARD,

OF DETROIT.

POEM.

LET Fancy fold her eager wings,
Let present cares and joys give way,
While Memory from her store-house brings
Visions that hold a surer sway.

Fling back the curtains of the past;
Just five-and-twenty years gone by,
I see beside this hallowed spot
A Master-Builder drawing nigh.

"Here will I build," I hear Him say,
"A glorious temple to My praise;
Foundation stones of colors fair
With precious stones thy walls I'll raise.

"And, first, that it unshaken stand—
The storms that round it beat, endure—
I'll lay beneath its massive walls
A Corner-Stone, well tried and sure—

"Thy walls the sapphire's brilliant blue;
Of glowing carbuncle thy gates;

Thy windows the pellucid light
  That on the crystal agate waits.

"Here great shall be thy children's peace —
  Terror and fear are born of guilt —
Taught of the Lord, thy children here
  In righteousness shall be upbuilt."

He spoke, and, lo, the building rose
  In fair proportions to my sight;
And when His Spirit was invoked
  His Presence filled it with delight.

Through all the changing years since first
  God met us, one by one,
Stone-pillowed, sleeping, careworn, lost,
  And called us for His own; —

Through sun and storm, through light and gloom
  Our Leader has been by,
Till now, divided in two bands,
  Our strength we multiply.

When God has chosen to remove
  For His own fairer courts above
Some prop our blindness would have kept,
  Has He not wrought the change with love?

And placed beneath the vacant spot,
That He might not our beauty mar,
Supports that fitted to their place,
Without the semblance of a jar?

Among those whom we are greeting
With mingled smiles and tears,
Are some whose hearts are swelling
With the thoughts of other years.

He who first, the Under-Shepherd,
Gathered in the flock with care,
Going in and out before them,
Seeking springs and pastures fair—

He who followed, rich in feeling,
Who the lambs so kindly led,
Skilfully the word divided,
And the sheep so wisely fed—

Who the one he held the dearest,
And the lamb his bosom knew,
Left amid your sacred sleepers,
Cherished tenderly by you;

Where the blossoms of each spring-time
Still by loving hands are strewn—
He to-night is weeping with you,
Ye who thought to weep alone.

But if we turn from earthly circles broken,
Faith's finger points to the bright home afar,
Where angel bands our ransomed ones have welcomed
To share a bliss which Death may never mar.

Oh, could we see the dim, half-polished jewel
Which here we fondly owned our fairest gem,
Freed from its clay, reset in heavenly splendor,
To sparkle in the Savior's diadem;

Might we not deem it almost selfish sorrow
To mourn our loss for such eternal gain;
Or learn, at least, from Faith's sweet light to borrow
A sacred solace for our bitter pain?

Here are others gladly welcomed,
Sharers of our hopes and fears,
Who have joined our sweet communion
In the days of other years.

They are marking still our bulwarks;
They are telling still our towers;
They our very dust are counting
Fairer than dew-laden flowers.

There are those to-night among us,
Tried helpers not a few,
To whom in one great volume
A shower of thanks is due.

And first we gladly mention
  Him who has kept good note
Of all the Church has witnessed—
  Each motion, act, and vote,

For a quarter of a century,
  With only thanks rewarded;
Each change of Pastors, Deacons, all
  By the same hand recorded.

Thanks to our TRUSTEES we offer,
  Always faithful in their calling,
Who, for credit and for safety,
  Keep our funds and spire from falling.

And next we thank the USHERS
  Whose constant joy has been
To welcome every stranger,
  And kindly take him in.

And next we thank the SINGERS,
  Whose skill our praise has won,
And the 'players upon instruments'
  Shall have our glad 'Well done!'

And we must bring our SEXTON
  Great share of our good will,
Though bowed beneath the weight of years
  A faithful worker still.

Thanks, too, for every LEADER
  Of our SABBATH SCHOOL is due,
And each TEACHER, from his store-house
  Bringing treasures old and new.

Leaving now the past behind us,
  Let us bring for future days
Richer offerings, sweeter incense,
  Nobler tributes to God's praise.

Then shall he who overcometh
  Stand beside the Emerald Throne,
Take, with new name written on it,
  From the King, a pure white stone:

And within that glorious City,
  Jasper-walled and garnished bright
With all manner of fair jewels,
  Flashing in celestial light;

He shall see the finished temple
  Perfect from the corner-stone,
And shall shout as he beholdeth,
  "Grace unto it, grace alone."

MEMORIAL ADDRESS,

BY

REV. H. D. KITCHEL, D.D.,

PRESIDENT OF MIDDLEBURY COLLEGE, VERMONT.

ADDRESS.

Thus far these Memorial services have simply borne the aspect of a glad thanksgiving for the signal favor of God towards this Church. We have traced with gratitude the leadings of a benign Providence in all the stages of its history. A Divine purpose has chosen its times and shaped its course, and we rejoice as we look back over the way in which we have been led, in the assurance that the supervision of a wise and loving Father has never failed us. We have marked with joy the same manifest grace which founded it still defending and sustaining it through the trials of its infancy; still building it into order and strength; ever watchfully ministering to its needs, and, above all, visiting it abundantly with the reviving and culture of the Divine Spirit. Thanks be to God this day that He gave this Church place and growth, and so speedily set it in favor and power among the Christian agencies in this city and State. "Hitherto hath the Lord helped us!" and well may we rejoice together with hearts full of gratitude as we review the history of this now-completed Quarter of a Century.

There remains now a service which has been deemed essential to this commemoration, which I have feared may bear a different aspect, and may seem to pitch itself on a key of regretful sadness. As far as we may, we make this a re-union of the Living Membership of this Church. With this large company of its present members, are assembled those who have gone from it to repeat its history in another part of the city; and many of us who shared, at one period or another, in its fortunes and labors, but have been thrown into other fields, gather back to-night to this dear old Home of our Hearts, and are here, one Church of the Living, to commemorate the Church of our Dead. We are met to remember those who through these years have parted from us at the summons of the Master; who, laying with us these foundations, and building for a time by our side, dropped, one by one, their earthly work and went on before us into the Church Triumphant. Remembering the dark day when they left us, and all our sense of loss, and how sorely we felt that we needed them here more than they could be needed in Heaven, it may seem only natural that such a Memorial service should cast itself in a mournful mood.

But I am persuaded that our second thought will go far to relieve this service from the tone of sadness. Nay, this is *not* the record of defeat! These are *not* the names of the fallen! Rather, this is a triumphal procession of the Victors! We rise by the warrant of our Christian Faith to commemorate our precious Dead as the very crown of our work and the seal of God's grace. If any of all these beloved graves have not been so washed with tears, if our hearts have not so yearned over them, as to prove the fulness of our grief and love, for such we may mourn to-night. But for those whom we have so loved and longed for, we will speak in the fit terms and tone of our Faith. We count these departed ones in reality the precious First-fruits of this Church Enterprise, the trophies of its achievement wherewith God has honored this Church. Let it be, then, with a serene and tempered gratitude, and with a sentiment of chastened triumph, that we commemorate now the souls that have here been trained and ripened in grace, and that have been called hence in their order to higher walks of service and joy in the Church of the Saved.

For is not this the very function of a Christian Church, the very end and purpose of its being, to nurture and train and perfect the souls of God's children; first of all to win them to Christ, and then to receive them as the heirs of life and handle them in all the gracious methods and appliances of a Christian nurture and education. Here, in the Church, the rude and shapeless masses, fresh from the quarry, are modeled and hewn into polished stones to enter by-and-by into the spiritual Temple above. For such space as pleases the Master, they are with us in training, under tuition, in the earthly Church. But their place is not here. They do but tarry here provisionally, and for a defined purpose, till they shall be nurtured for their true place and ultimate service; and when they have reached that point, their education is completed, and they are summoned home. It is, indeed, the sore trial of our faith when these ripe souls depart. Ah! how the black cloud of this sorrow, never long absent, goes shifting around this congregation, from slip to slip, symbolizing with its dark drapery the hearts that are bleeding beneath! How can we spare them? And the fitter they are to go the less we can spare them! God's work here so needs them and just when ripe and on the wing for Heaven, Earth wants them most, and we bewail them with deepest regret. Ah! if Heaven were to wait for our consent — if none might pass to it till our suffrage dismissed them, when would they ever be spared from us! God only is the competent Judge. He knows His own perfect purpose in each redeemed soul, and when each has come to that stage of completeness which fits it for just the place and work designed for it, wisely, but sovereignly, the fiat comes, and they are gone from us, having their place henceforth among the Immortals.

My brethren, it is of God's wisdom, doubtless, that our eyes should be so holden that we should see only in part, and so in our blindness bewail as our uttermost sorrow what is hailed of the angels as a commemoration of joy. What we call Death, and count for our bitterest grief, they hail as in reality the clearing of Life from all its obstructions, the birth of a soul into more abundant Life.

> We call this *Life;* but Life's a name
> That nothing here can truly claim.
> This wretched Inn where we scarce stay to bait
> We call our *dwelling-place!*
> We call one step a race!
> But angels in their full enlightened state,
> Angels who *live* and know what 'tis *to be*,
> Who all the nonsense of our language see,
> Who speak *things*, and our words and ill-drawn pictures scorn,
> When we by a foolish figure say,
> "*Behold an old man dead,*" — then they
> Speak properly, and say, "BEHOLD A MAN-CHILD BORN."

And just then while we mourn, heartbroken, and fill the air with wailings for our dead, they crowd with glad expectance on the other shore to welcome another immortal and crown with amaranth one more life begun! We will not complain of this salutary blindness. Death must needs be to us a riddle mis-read. We could not bear to be wise. The Sphinx must hold its secret, in tragic and stony mystery, inexorable because merciful to the questioning of mortals. To open our eyes on this one point, and give us to comprehend Death, would involve an utter revolution in the whole scheme and process of our earthly life. A child must be childish and grope toward the light through illusions, and climb by half-knowledge to the wholeness of Truth. The glass we must yet see through darkens all, warps very much, and some things inverts. And Death is one of these inverted images — our own death, and that of those dear friends — and just as we must needs be tied to our life, each one by a blind, unreasoning, often unreasonable, instinctive passion for living, so we must needs clasp those we love, and passionately hold them down with us by the uttermost tug of our hearts, blindly, and feeling as our keenest sorrow what is, to every son of God, his birth into Immortal Life.

And yet we do suspect the truth even in the agony of our grief. Thanks be to God! as we gaze upward in faith, almost we see through our tears that it is well the good should die. A little our eyes are opened. The dawn of Immortality begins to make twilight around the grave, shining more and more, till we cry, "Oh Death! this was victory which we thought defeat!" and presently, when "afterwards the peaceable fruits" appear, we begin to consent to the Divine wisdom and goodness of Death, and see that when the full corn is in the ear, it ought to go to the garner.

It is to be well considered, too, in estimating the influence of this blindness which happens to us on the whole matter of Death, how largely it serves to the needed trial of our faith and discipline of grace. Perhaps not another element enters more deeply into Christian culture than that of sorrow and trial from the dispensation of Death. Here it is our faith in God is tested and developed. Here resignation, fortitude, and all that group of kindred graces, have scope and culture. Far more than we are wont to think, the effective tuition of Character in all the more robust and hardy virtues, comes of that feature in God's economy which wraps from mortal apprehension the mystery of Death.

With this juster view, we gain the true criterion of the efficiency of a Christian Church, the measure of the real service it has rendered, and of the Divine honor which has been put upon it, namely, this: How many souls of God's saints has it trained and graduated into the Church of the Redeemed in glory? Those yet left in it here are souls in their infancy, under tutelage, still encompassed by infirmity and marred by defect — candidates, racers still on the course, amid the agony and hazard of an unfinished race. But they whom the Father hath taken home are finished products, forever secure. The ripe fruits are gathered into the garner. These are so many trophies of victory achieved, the golden wheat ripened, reaped and winnowed from these seed-fields of the Lord in His earthly Church, the harvests they have been blessed and honored to bear to the glory of God's grace. The husbandman, as he watches in the spring-time the seed just shooting from the soil, has indeed the joy of hope — and a still bolder trust when summer gives ripening promise of the harvest — and yet more confident joy when the yellow fields begin to beckon the reaper — but it is a joy mingled at every stage with fear, and tempered by his sense of many a peril. But with what serene and happy security he shows you the gathered sheaves, the full fruits safely garnered at last! Our garnered fruits are those whom we call our lost ones — in truth, *our only safe ones!* And it should not be beyond our faith to-day to rise to the height of a serene and tempered joy, as we count up the souls that have risen from our number, year by year, through this Quarter of a Century, and passed into the presence and service of the Lord.

Yes, verily, the very crown of honor on this beloved Church is, its fruitfulness in souls ripened for the Kingdom. And already what riches it has, laid up beyond all hazard! And as the years roll on, and, name by name, God calls His own, and our jewels go from us to be set in the diadem of the King, we will comfort our sadness by sharing, as we may, in the joy that is felt among the angels of God. And as this dear Church grows old, as one after another the Quarter-Centuries go by — as this company of our Dead, whom we tenderly commemorate to-night, shall welcome us and our successors to their growing number, how venerable, how precious and honorable, this Church shall become, still yielding its large harvests of ripened souls, well known in Heaven as one of its feeders, and watched of all the expectant hosts above for the ample income it yields to their ranks. Mother and Nurse of Souls! what a company of her children are gathering already there, graduates of this school of grace, still holding it in dear remembrance and fond regard, and watching to welcome us who still linger below!

Yes, tenderly they remember this scene of their earthly training, and yearn with affectionate interest toward this spot consecrated by their conflict and victory. I seem to speak even now in another presence than yours whom I see, as one compassed at this moment by another company whom our eyes may not behold. An assembly of the Unseen seems to gird us around; a silent concourse, claiming their places, with no token of their coming save to that inner sense by which we know and feel them near. We know not, indeed, the conditions of that higher Life now theirs: but if, as we trust, it be within the permitted franchises of the redeemed ever to revisit the scenes of their earthly course, surely that company of dear souls gone before draw near to-night, and share with us the memories that swell our hearts. They who through all these years dropped, one by one, from our side — the faces that looked up to me from these seats — they are here, not less than the faces I see. Almost their well-remembered voices greet our ears, and the clasp of their hands seems warm in our palms to-night. Was it not yesterday they trod these aisles with us and sat with us in these slips? Years have scarce dimmed the freshness of the joy we had in their living, and the anguish that wrung our hearts when the grave shut them from our sight. It cannot be but that it is given them to know very much that passes here on earth, much of all that touches God's glory in the Church and in us, whom they can never cease to love. And if it be so, we need no other assurance that they are with us now, and that they mingle with our emotions the gladness and the congratulations of all those who have gone from this Church to the Church Triumphant.

Looking forward to this occasion, I have turned over, page by page, and year by year, my records and my memories, and lived over again, scene by scene, the sixteen years of my Pastorate with this Church. Strange record, as of some pre-existence, it starts into fresh life, all aglow with its rapid changes—its love, joy, trial, pathos! I despair of reproducing these memories in any fit and adequate terms. With this Roll of our Beloved and Honored Dead—this List of our Promoted — with these Nine and Fifty Names of those dying while I was with you -- with these, and the memories that cluster around each name — what can I worthily do? Others more recent and fresh in your remembrance, who have gone from your number since November, 1864, will be appropriately commemorated by your present Pastor. Briefly I will speak of those whose departure I witnessed.

My ministry among you commenced in the

autumn of 1848 — my first Sabbath October 1st of that year, and my installation the 6th of December following. The first work had been done in gathering and organizing this Church, and the trials incident to the infancy of such an enterprise had, in good measure, been passed under the care of my predecessor, Rev. HENRY L. HAMMOND, to whose faithful and self-denying labors this Church owes a debt of honor and gratitude. Under him, by God's favor, this Church had settled its first three-sided question, that *it ought to be* — that *it could be* — and that *it was*. It was fairly entered in the field which it has since occupied. But its numbers and strength were yet small, and the members of the Church and the families which made up its Congregation were scattered quite widely over the city.

I recall only a single death — that of Miss ANN McLEOD, from our number, until the following summer of 1849. In that season the cholera appeared, and for a few days wrought quite fatally among us. It was my first acquaintance with that terrible disease. Miami avenue seemed the center of its ravages, and, for a short time, the alarm in that street and the vicinity rose nearly to a panic. The sick, or dying, or dead, were in nearly every house. Many fled, and the faith and firmness of all were severely tested. The older members of this Church will recall that season of alarm, and the death of brother R. W. WARNER. His was a loss severely felt in our then feeble condition, and one which, from his character and worth, was deeply deplored.

The same season took from us Mrs. MARY A. WARREN, CATHARINE BATES, and JOSEPH A. CHRISTIE; and brother WILLIAM T. AVERY died in the following spring. FANNY VAN TASSEL and Mrs. ELIZABETH T. SHAW left us in 1851, and the next year was made memorable by four deaths of members, each bringing us its especial burden of grief. Our venerable father LUDDEN dropped all infirmity and was crowned with immortal youth. Brother GEORGE COMMON left the memory of an eminently faithful and prayerful man. Mrs. BAGG — the CELIA M. BALDWIN, whose personal loveliness and refined Christian excellence gave such beauty to her life and so much sadness to her early death — left us in June; and in August, far away in his California sojourn, brother NATHANIEL T. TAYLOR was struck down by cholera. The burden of that bereavement is scarcely lightened yet among us by the seventeen years since he went to his distant grave.

The next season opened with many stricken families and swept from us in succession Mrs. NANCY WATKINS, brother WILLIAM F. STEVENS, Mrs. KETURAH C. JAMES, Mrs. SARAH PARK, Mrs. ANN

Eliza Guile, Miss Mary Bissell, and John M. TenEycke.

To many of you, the following names will sadly recall the second visitation of cholera in 1854, more afflictive to me as most of them died during my absence abroad. The hand of God seemed heavy on us, while, one after another, James H. Green, William Hamlyn, Charles Hall, and B. M. Sheldon fell in our foremost ranks, and when the ripe dignity of Mrs. Eunice E. Bates, and the gracious Christian ladyhood of Mrs. Hetty Monds went from us. And to these were added in the next year the names of Mrs. Jane Common, and Mrs. Noble. In 1856, our losses were peculiarly trying. Mrs. Maria Wilkins—what a shock of agony tore that gentle spirit from us! and the anguish, so swiftly renewed, when Frances Nall bore away with her the flower of young wifely and motherly grace to bloom in the Garden of the King. Brother Perkins, was soon added to these; and our beloved young brother, Edward S. Tyler, went soon to the Savior in the freshness of his first love. And in the following year the father went, brother Elisha Tyler; and Mrs. Mary Rice closed in great peace a long life of vicissitude.

On that sad roll of widowhood and orphanage and broken homes, which has grown so numerous among us, many names were written in the dark mo ths of 1858. The names of Mrs. MARY ANDERSON, Mrs. CHARLES BRADLEY, Mrs. ANN S. KITCHEL, Mrs. MELVINA MESSENGER, and Mrs. BETSY W. RICE, will sufficiently recall that year of trial. And the tide of sorrow rose still in the succeeding year and added many precious names to the list of our memorable dead. Out of the furnace of long pain, GEORGE HOLMES entered at last into incorruptible youth. CELESTIA A. POWELL followed — a maiden of rare loveliness and Christian experience. Mrs. ADALINE BULL, and Mrs. MARY BULL, followed these. Then came that mystery of bitter suffering and madness, in which Mrs. FRANCES C. MURRAY broke her way out of her miseries, we trust, into heavenly reason and rest. And as I name these four, Mrs. ELECTA DIMMICK, Mrs. HARRIET B. WARNER, Mrs. EMILY STEBBINS, and Mrs. MARIA L. WHEATON, our aching hearts feel. almost as keenly as we felt in the depth of that great darkness in which they left us, at what cost of our dearest and best Heaven grows so rich! Our other sister, Mrs. HORACE WHEATON, went soon after, and Mrs. HESTER BODMAN, and brother SQUIRE W. PATCHEN. Mrs. MARY SANFORD died May 8, 1862. THOMAS FARRELL left a memory very precious and imperishable among us. His bright promise, his devoted piety and manly worth, his mysterious and sudden death, and the anguish of his broken home, give him a mournful distinction in the annals of this Church.

We have also our Roll of Honor. We, too, as a Church, paid part in the price of blood for our delivered Country. Brother WILLIAM BLISS was captured in service at Corinth, and wantonly slain at Montgomery, in Alabama, in July, 1862; and in the same season Dr. DWIGHT STEBBINS fell by disease while rendering professional service after the bloody days of Shiloh and Pittsburg Landing. We received back only the remains of our brother HERBERT ADAMS, dying in the service; and Major HENRY W. NALL returned only to linger for a season and die of a malady contracted in the service. And in this list, though not of our membership, Capt. CHARLES J. SNIDER and EDWIN M. CONKLIN should have honorable record.

Of those still living who stood for us at the front, and bore our hearts and prayers on many a bloody field, worthy mention has already been made by our historian. But their names can never too often be repeated. LANE. WORMER, SWIFT, and NALL—TROWBRIDGE, RICE, RAYMOND and CURTIS — THOMPSON and HARTER — ACKER and ACKER — they did our work, and shall never lack our honor that they did it well, nor our gladness that they did it and lived.

Early in 1863, we parted with our beloved sister Mrs. RUTH LANE. Death gives us many and varied lessons. It was reserved for our sister, Mrs. C. I. WALKER, in the ripeness of a serene and steadfast faith, to show us how a Christian, through pain and slow decay, can face and wait and welcome the sure and well-known coming of death. The names of Mrs. BARROWS, and Mrs. CAROLINE E. WHITWOOD close the record of those dying during my pastorate, from the membership of this Church.

Over all these sixteen years are scattered thickly the recorded deaths of dear children. Evermore the Savior has stretched His arms toward us and cried, "Suffer the little children to come unto Me!" Ah! the Kingdom is full of such! In their fresh brightness they pass away unstained, like the dew-drops of a summer morning at the first look of the sun. Ever the souls of our sweet little ones are rising as an exhalation from Earth to Heaven, while our fond, yearning hearts follow heavenward this flight of our fireside angels. They hid their wings from us as they lay on our bosom for a time, till we almost deemed them our own — then, suddenly, at the Master's call, they lifted their pinions and soared homeward! I have before me a long list of these dearly cherished names. KITTIE HOWARD, FREDDIE and EDDIE HOLMES, WILLIE NOBLE, MATTIE WALCOTT, CHARLIE EDWARDS, little ANNIE,* WILLIE PARSONS, MARIA PARTRIDGE, JENNIE BARNARD, MARY HALL, KITTIE DUNCKLEE, EBEN and EMMIE RUSSELL, FREDDIE ADAMS, KITTIE RICE, EMMIE CLOUGH, WILLIE CASE, KITTIE ACKER, NANCY HIBBARD, FRANKIE BIGELOW, EMMIE JONES, FRANKIE and CHARLIE ADAMS, FRANKIE BAKER, GEORGIE BOSTWICK, CHARLIE HOLMES, LIZZIE and EMMIE KING, MINNIE LAPHAM, JOHN S. HITTEL, EFFIE WALKER, little OPHELIA,* FREDDIE TARBELL, WILLIE and JENNIE KEITH, GEORGE CAREY, LEVERETT DUDLEY BACKUS, SUSIE SELDEN, JOSEPH HOWARD HILDRETH, JOHN JAMES.

Gladly would I commemorate others, not a few, once members with us, who have been removed, and died in other fields; Mrs. MARY J. HAMMOND, Dea. CHARLES HOWARD, Mrs. MARY TILLMAN, JOSEPH C. BAILEY and ROBERT PURDY and wife. Of these, one name deserves to be tenderly recalled by us — that of Dea. CHARLES HOWARD, whose prayers and faith entered deeply into all the spiritual history of this Church. He left us in 1861, and five years later, it was my joy to possess him

*Daughters of the speaker.

again in my Church in Chicago. A little later, God called him home by a fatal hurt received in the discharge of his duty on a railroad. And others still, not members of our Church, but intimately associated with its interests and prized for their noble worth, or tenderly held in our Christian solicitudes — such names as those of CHARLES AVERY, JEDEDIAH HIBBARD, JOHN B. DAVIS, Rev. EBENEZER COLMAN, GOVERNOR and Mrs. WILLIAM WOODBRIDGE, WILLIAM H. RUSSELL, Mrs. J. P. CLARK, Mrs. LIBBIE BUTLER, Mrs. FLETCHER, D. P. BUSHNELL, Mrs. OPHELIA S. KITCHEL and GEORGE F. PORTER. And still another class compels remembrance — that group of dear youth whose early death still saddens our homes — Mrs. HENRY NALL, ALFRED MINER, Miss ALICE HULBERT, young BISSELL and NEWHALL, Mrs. DELPHINE CUTTER, Mrs. CHAS. TOWN, Miss FLORINE TEFT, GEORGE COOK, RICHMOND HOLMES, WILSON BROOKS, and SHERMAN BARNARD. Pardon me if I linger among these sacred memories. Name by name, what histories rush on my thought, what forms start freshly to life, as if the utterance of their names to-night were a spell stronger than the grave, and gave them back to us for a little space, to appease the hunger of our hearts.

It remains that we gratefully record one other, the most central and crowning favor of God toward

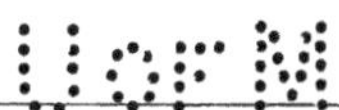

this Church. It will most fitly close this Memorial to remember now with devoutest gratitude the precious scenes of Reviving Grace that crowned these critical years of our history. Many souls were born to Christ among us.* In the early months of 1848, under the special labors of Rev. J. T. Avery, many had indulged hope of renewal, and sixty-one were added to us in the course of the year, many of whom united with us soon after I assumed the pastorate. In 1851 the gracious work was repeated with happy and very abundant fruit, and I have assurance that about seventy of the converts of

---

*I find from my records that additions were made to the Church, year by year, as follows:

In 1844,	by letter and profession,	22
" 1845,	" "	42
" 1846,	" "	22
" 1847,	" "	31
" 1848,	" "	61
" 1849,	" "	20
" 1850,	" "	22
" 1851,	" "	61
" 1852,	" "	30
" 1853,	" "	21
" 1854,	" "	13
" 1855,	" "	49
" 1856,	" "	55
" 1857,	" "	34
" 1858,	" "	74
" 1859,	" "	27
" 1860,	" "	13
" 1861,	" "	17
" 1862,	" "	31
" 1863,	" "	17
		662

The number who joined in 1864, I cannot state.

Of the original thirteen who formed this Church, December 25, 1844, there are now in its living membership, Dea. Lyman Baldwin and wife, Dea. Barnard, Dea. Francis Raymond and wife, Brother William Cook and wife, Mrs. Robert Warner, and Miss Rhoda Cowles.

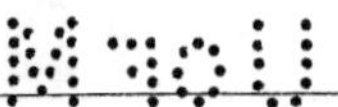

that revival were added to this and other Churches. Again, in 1855, through all the spring and summer, we rejoiced in a continued and deep-working revival, and that season and the following added 104 to our number, in large part the fruits of that gracious harvest. In that year of signal grace, 1858, when a peculiar spiritual activity was witnessed very widely in the Churches, and when the power of a quickened and devoted lay agency was singularly developed, this Church shared long and largely in that happy impulse, and seventy-four were that season gathered to our fold. These were our chief harvest seasons; but at least three other gracious quickenings were granted us, with considerable product of renewed souls, deserving our grateful remembrance. In all, as nearly as I can gather, from the organization to the time of my leaving, we received six hundred and seventy-three to our membership, of whom a large proportion were of those hopefully renewed among us, and many others, born here, found homes in other Churches.

This, then, is our Memorial before God. After this manner, "hitherto hath the Lord helped us." Dear Church of my early love and fondest hope! Dear Flock, the scene of my best years and sweetest toils and dearest affections, my joy and the crown of my life-work, if any God's grace shall give me in heaven! Dear Church of Christ's love and care! precious to so many pleading hearts that still yearn toward it on the earth, and precious to so many who watch you from the other shore, with ministries of sympathy and undying tenderness beyond all we can know! Dear Company of God's own, to you now, and to this honored man of God, your Pastor, we bequeath this Inheritance of prayers and toils, this History of God's Grace, this unfinished Work of the Lord. God grant you a Future that shall fulfil the Past! Build well and faithfully on these foundations. Many of us will not be seen with you in the flesh when you celebrate your Semi-Centennial. But I think we shall be here. Long ere that day comes round, a still larger company of us will have joined that band already gathered on high, caring evermore and tenderly, even in Heaven, for this dear Mother, and Nurse, and Home of our souls.

MEMORIAL ADDRESS,

BY

REV. SAMUEL M. FREELAND,

OF DETROIT.

ADDRESS.

It is with very great reluctance that I mention before you the names of those who died among you after the dismission of your former Pastor, and before the coming of your present one. Some of these I did not know at all, some of them but slightly, and almost all of them must have been better known to you and to my predecessor than to myself.

In November, 1864, Mr. J. H. Carpenter, a member of this Church, passed away from earth. A few days since we followed to their resting place beside her father's remains, those of his youngest daughter, Mrs. Stewart, the first of his family to rejoin him.

In December, 1864, on the day before my arrival in Detroit, died Mr. C. L. Safford. He left behind him a reputation for business integrity and Christian character more precious than gold to those that loved him.

Two months later, Death came to a family where

he was then no stranger, and where he has twice since crossed the threshold, and called out of the congregation Mr. JONATHAN EDWARDS, the oldest son of his widowed mother. In his sickness and death there was a blessing upon him and upon those he left behind him.

In that same month of February, 1865, the Lord sent His messenger for two others, members of this Church. Mr. SERENO C. HAMMOND, brother of Hon. CHARLES G. and Rev. HENRY L. HAMMOND, came to his rest after a long, and, at the last, very painful illness. He closed a manly life with a Christian death. His daughter, ISABEL, who clung to him with a peculiar and fully reciprocated fondness, has, within a few months, followed him to the land of rest. Mrs. JANE T. CARVER, wife of Mr. DAVID CARVER, died of an attack of malignant erysipelas. A lady of brilliant parts and captivating manners, her death left vacant a place in the Church and in the social circles of her every-day life, which her friends felt it would not be easy to fill.

On the day in which tidings had come to us of the assassination of President LINCOLN, April 15th, 1865, we bore to his burial Mr. HENRY ARNOLD, who had passed away more suddenly than the President. In almost usual health, he had gone from his home to his business, and at his work fell dead upon the floor. An unobtrusive but decided Christian, his prompt response to the sudden call to a higher work, must have been given with great joy, though he left in his earthly home a great sorrow.

In the month following, an infant daughter of Mr. and Mrs. ERVIN PALMER, was taken up out of loving arms by loving angels, for the Lord had bidden them do it.

In the same month, May, 1865, died Mr. CHARLES C. TYLER, one of the young business men of the city, whose energy and Christian character gave promise of success and usefulness in the future; but consumption had marked him for a victim, as, just one year later, in May, 1866, the same disease brought his wife, Mrs. ELISABETH C. TYLER, to lie beside him in the "city of the dead," as it already had sent thither, three months after his departure, his sister, Miss SUSANNA TYLER, who had vainly sought health by a sojourn in England, and who at last met the Lord's messenger at Warwick, R. I. These three had all been members of this Church for a number of years, and in the early prime of manhood and womanhood, they entered the Church Above. Sweet are the memories they have left to those that loved them.

The four weeks of my vacation absence in July and August, 1865, were a time of especial enriching of the Family in Heaven with those taken from the bosom of this "Mother and Nurse of souls." Mrs. DEBORAH C. NASH, mother-in-law of Mr. JAMES NALL, Jr.; Mrs. LAURA A. SELDEN, wife of Mr. J. G. SELDEN; Mrs. GEORGE WINTER, whose sweetly-chastened little daughter soon followed her to rest; the infant children of Mr. and Mrs. JOHN A. WILKES, Mr. and Mrs. A. D. PIERCE, and Hon. and Mrs. WILLIAM WARNER, these all passed away in those weeks, leaving vacant seats, and empty arms, and aching hearts behind them—places all their own, which will never quite be filled by others.

In October, 1865, little JENNY NILES passed quickly away, the water of parental baptism lying almost fresh upon her brow.

In the December following, FLORA ALICE GEER, at the age of fourteen years, eldest daughter of Mrs. R. GEER, seemed to take the hand of her Savior and go away with Him to walk in the light.

In November of that same autumn, there came to die among us Deacon MILLER, of the then newly-formed Congregational Church of Alpena. He had stopped on his journey to the East, to spend a few days with his daughter, Mrs. GEORGE N. FLETCHER, when Death met him. He fell as the veteran falls, with his harness upon him.

In the early spring of 1866, at the beginning of March, the Lord came for his long-tried, anxiously-waiting servant, Mrs. CATHARINE A. HOWARD, wife of Hon. JACOB M. HOWARD. Richly endowed with gifts of nature and of grace; fitted fully for her position as wife, and mother, and friend, and Christian worker; her family, and friends, and the Church could ill spare her from among them, but the answer to their questioning grief, as they saw her fading, as the consumptive fades, was only this: "What I do, thou knowest not now; but thou shalt know hereafter."

Two months later, when the flowers were coming, and the song birds told of newness of life on the earth, there was newness of life in the land of endless spring for another of our number, Miss JENNY SMITH, second daughter of Mr. and Mrs. R. C. SMITH. Sweetly she fell on sleep, and, we doubt not, sweetly awoke where they slumber not any more.

"Blessed are they that do His commandments, that they may have right to the tree of life, and may enter in through the gates into the city."

MEMORIAL ADDRESS,

BY

REV. ADDISON BALLARD, D.D.,

OF DETROIT.

ADDRESS.

Continuing this roll of the departed ones, the first name recorded by the present Pastor, is that of Mrs. James Holmes, of Waterbury, Conn., who came hither an invalid, hoping for restored health in the atmosphere of the lakes. Disappointed in this, on her return from Marquette, she found a home and ministrations of Christian sympathy with her relative, Mrs. S. M. Hibbard, until she was taken to her rest, June 12, 1866.

August 31. On the last day of the same summer, we laid away in Elmwood, the form of Florence Bostwick; and on the last day of the spring following, May 31, 1867, we laid by her side her infant sister, little Belle Ashley. The God of Abraham, Isaac, and Jacob, the God, not of the Dead, but of the Living, will one day tell the thrice-stricken parents why He sometimes gathers our fairest lilies so soon, and why He gathers so many from one garden.

October 23. THOMAS W. BISSELL. This precious young man God took, as we believe, from the imperfections of earth to the home of the pure and gentle-hearted in Heaven.

November 3. Mr. and Mrs. E. MINER CLARK lost a dearly-beloved son, RICHMOND HOLMES, at the age of four years.

December 7. Mrs. N. G. WILLIAMS. Not forgetting in health the things that are unseen and eternal, she went forward to meet them, leaning on the Savior whom she loved, and whom it was her desire to confess before men by uniting openly with his people. On the 25th of the month following, she received again to her embrace, the infant daughter, a few weeks old, to whose life she had given her own.

December 11. Hon. CHAUNCEY GRIGGS died at the house of his son-in-law, Mr. G. O. WILLIAMS. Two years previous, he removed to Detroit from Tolland, Conn., where the various public trusts committed to him for a long course of years evinced the confidence which his fellow citizens reposed in him as a man of sound judgment and incorruptible integrity.

THE YEAR 1867.

March 20. Mrs. MARY LEONARD RICE, who died in Washington, D. C., was buried from Westminster church in this city, where, less than six months before, she had given and received the vows of plighted love at the bridal altar.

March 31. Mrs. MARY DAVIS. She manifested in a striking manner her great love for the public worship of God, by her faithful attendance in the sanctuary, notwithstanding severe bodily afflictions.

April 15. This day witnessed the beautiful end of a beautiful life in the passing away of ISABEL R. ADAMS, whom her Lord lovingly took from great and prolonged suffering, patiently borne, to fullness of joy in His own presence, to the pleasures which are at His right hand forevermore.

May 25. Mrs. GEORGE W. BARNARD died at St. Clair. From her youth she had been a member of this Church, and was highly esteemed and tenderly beloved by all with whom she was brought into intimate companionship, for the steady and undimmed brightness of the quiet, consistent and faithful Christian example which she displayed to all who took knowledge of her that she had learned of Jesus. Her early departure saddened many hearts.

June 21. WILLIAM PURDY, once a member of this Church, during his last days expressed a greatly revived tenderness of affection for the Church of his earlier years, and passed away in the peace of a re-awakened penitence, and of renewed trust in the mercy of his Redeemer.

July 23. Captain and Mrs. Robert J. Hackett were afflicted in the loss of an infant daughter by the summer scourge of children; and, one month later,

August 22, Mr. and Mrs. Newell Avery sustained a like bereavement in the death of a little daughter of like age, and by the same malady.

November 24. Mr. Russell A. Coe died at the house of his sister, Mrs. S. M. Hibbard. An expected reunion of friends under this sister's roof, after long and wide separation, gave the prospect of an unusually happy winter. But the first congratulations were scarcely over ere the shadows of this affliction began to darken. The heart was saddened just as it was most buoyant with hope. The ashes were cold on the hearthstone just as we neared the borders of that time when, of all the year, the fires of domestic love are wont to glow most brightly.

THE YEAR 1868.

May 15. Maggie P. Brooks. With everything at her disposal to make life desirable here, she cheerfully resigned all for that Eternal Life which is the gift of God to the believer through Jesus

Christ our Lord. Finding Christ in prayer, in His Word, in the broken bread and poured wine of the Supper, in the communion of Christian hearts, she did not want, she did not fear. Her cup overflowed.

May 30. HENRY HOWE, an affectionate son and brother, in his friendships singularly strong and steadfast.

July 29. Hon. WILLIAM WARNER died in Quincy, Illinois, while superintending the erection of an iron bridge over the Mississippi. Notwithstanding Mr. WARNER's rare gifts and attainments, his great grasp and reach of intellect, the crown and radiance of his character was his Christian humility. A few days before his death, he said, in the self-distrust of conscious weakness and imperfection, but at the same time in the joy of a calm trust in Jesus, "In many things I have come short of my duty, but the Lord is my Shepherd. If it were the Lord's will, I should be glad to live, that I might *round out my life* by giving myself more earnestly to prayer, and the study of His Word." But his work was done. While viewing from the window of his sick chamber, with the help of a field glass, the progress of the noble structure spanning the mighty Father of Waters, an airy link in one of the great highways of the Continent to bind its two ocean shores together, angel-builders were silently laying the beams of that mysterious crossing, hidden from mortal eye, over which the feet of God's released pilgrims pass to the Heavenly Shore.

July 31 and August 11. Little HELEN and JULIA, twin daughters, but a few weeks old, of Mr. and Mrs. ALFRED HOWARD. Will they ever know any other birthplace but Heaven?

August 22. Mr. and Mrs. CHRISTIAN MELLUS were deeply afflicted by the drowning, in Detroit river, of a son of eight years of age.

October 17. RUSSELL A. HIBBARD. The friends most intimately acquainted with his inner life, had seen, for some time before his death, how God was leading this dear boy in "paths of righteousness" and Christian peace, but, alas, they little thought that it was because he was so soon to walk without fear by the side of the Good Shepherd, through the shadows of the Dark Valley.

November 17. In the unlooked-for departure of Mrs. H. W. STANDART, Sen., while her husband and a large circle of children mourn one of the best of wives and mothers, they are comforted by memories of her exemplary life, and the tranquility with which she met an exchange of worlds.

November 22. Mr. HUGH H. WRIGHT, after a protracted and very painful illness, which we cannot but hope was blessed to his convers on and salvation.

November 24. CHARLES W. KEITH, son of Mrs. G. W. LATIMER, aged ten years, whose love for the Bible, and the Sunday School, and Christian hymns, gave good reason to believe that, prepared by the Holy Spirit, his young heart, as good ground, had already received the good seed of the Kingdom.

December 20. Mrs. D. M. RICHARDSON. During her illness, her mind dwelt with peculiar pleasure on that beautiful scene, where, in the form of a dove, purity, gentleness, and peace, driven from the world by sin, came to it again in the person and through the work of the Lord Jesus Christ. On the Lord's day, the heavens opened to receive the spirit of this now sainted sister, who breathes the pure and peaceful atmosphere of that same Heaven where Jesus is.

THE YEAR 1869.

January 2. At this date we lost another of the most faithful of our members, Mrs. E. D. JONES. She loved the ordinances of God's house, and it was a great solace to her in her sickness that, when in health, she had never failed in her attendance on the means of grace.

March 25. In the death of Mrs. ABBY P. COLMAN, who died in Princeton, Ill., but was brought hither for interment, the deep grief of her children at the loss of so precious a mother was mingled with so much of thanksgiving that she had so long been spared to them, that they found it easy to say: "Blessed be the name of Him who gave and who has taken away."

April 5. ISABEL HAMMOND. It seemed strange to us that one so well fitted by sanctified intelligence and culture for Christian usefulness in so many places, should be removed from us; that a light which shone with so much purity and constancy in the Church, in the Sunday School, and in the family, should be so soon extinguished. But in the light of that higher service to which the Master has called her, it no longer seems strange to her; it will not long seem strange to us.

April 30. Mrs. THOMAS MURPHY. The unfeigned and deep sorrow which the death of this dear friend occasioned here, evinced how tenderly she had endeared herself to those who had been happy enough to know her well. Her presence was a blessing in the Sunday School, whether as Teacher or as a member of the Bible Class, in the prayer meeting, and in the social circle. As her Pastor, I cannot recall without a pang of regret for my great loss, the pleasant and affectionate manner with which she uniformly greeted me whenever and wherever we met. So perfectly did she seem to understand the manifold engrossments of a Pastor's time and thoughts, as to convey the impression that she took more pleasure in looking after *him*, than she would take in the feeling that he must be looking after *her*. This was due to her beautiful spirit of self-forgetfulness, enhanced, doubtless, by the experience gained by being reared in a Pastor's home. She was the daughter of Rev. J. A. THOME, of Cleveland, Ohio.

July 12. Mr. and Mrs. ALBERT D. PIERCE were called, a second time, to taste the bitterness of affliction in burying an only child, their beloved JENNIE, at the age of seven months.

August 19. Mrs. Rev. JAMES NALL closed a life of active, ardent piety which had proved a rich blessing to multitudes, first in England, the place of her nativity, subsequently in Canada, and, later still, within the bounds of our own State. Hers is the blessed memory of the just.

September 20. Mr. WILLIAM B. COLBURN, after a distressing illness of eighteen months. I do not remember ever to have met with a more marked case of sanctified affliction. Scarcely had God sent his arrows, before He came after with the precious balm of consolation. He felt that God was not against him, but with him in his affliction, calling him to a more earnest attention to the things of salvation, to come back to the Savior from whom he confessed that the engrossments of business had caused him to stray. He heard this call, but found, as he expressed it, that our Heavenly Father does not wait for his son's return, but runs out to meet and embrace him, and to welcome him home.

October 22. With the name of our latest departed, TURNER STETSON, this Memorial Record is closed, and closed most worthily. This dear brother was one of God's noblemen, a wonderful trophy of His transforming grace; one who ever found a home in the Church, because he came forward manfully and made himself at home in it; a man of whom an intimate friend and keen discerner of character once said: "I know of no man in the city of Detroit, whose life for the last thirty years has been so uniformly consistent."

Dear Friends of the Church and Congregation: The list of those of our number who have finished their earthly trial and gone to their account is ended. The cloud of witnesses, at first no larger than a man's hand, is overspreading the heavens. Very soon for each one of us the record will be closed and sealed up forever. Let us, with all diligence, earnestness and promptitude, finish, and finish well, the work which God has given us to do.

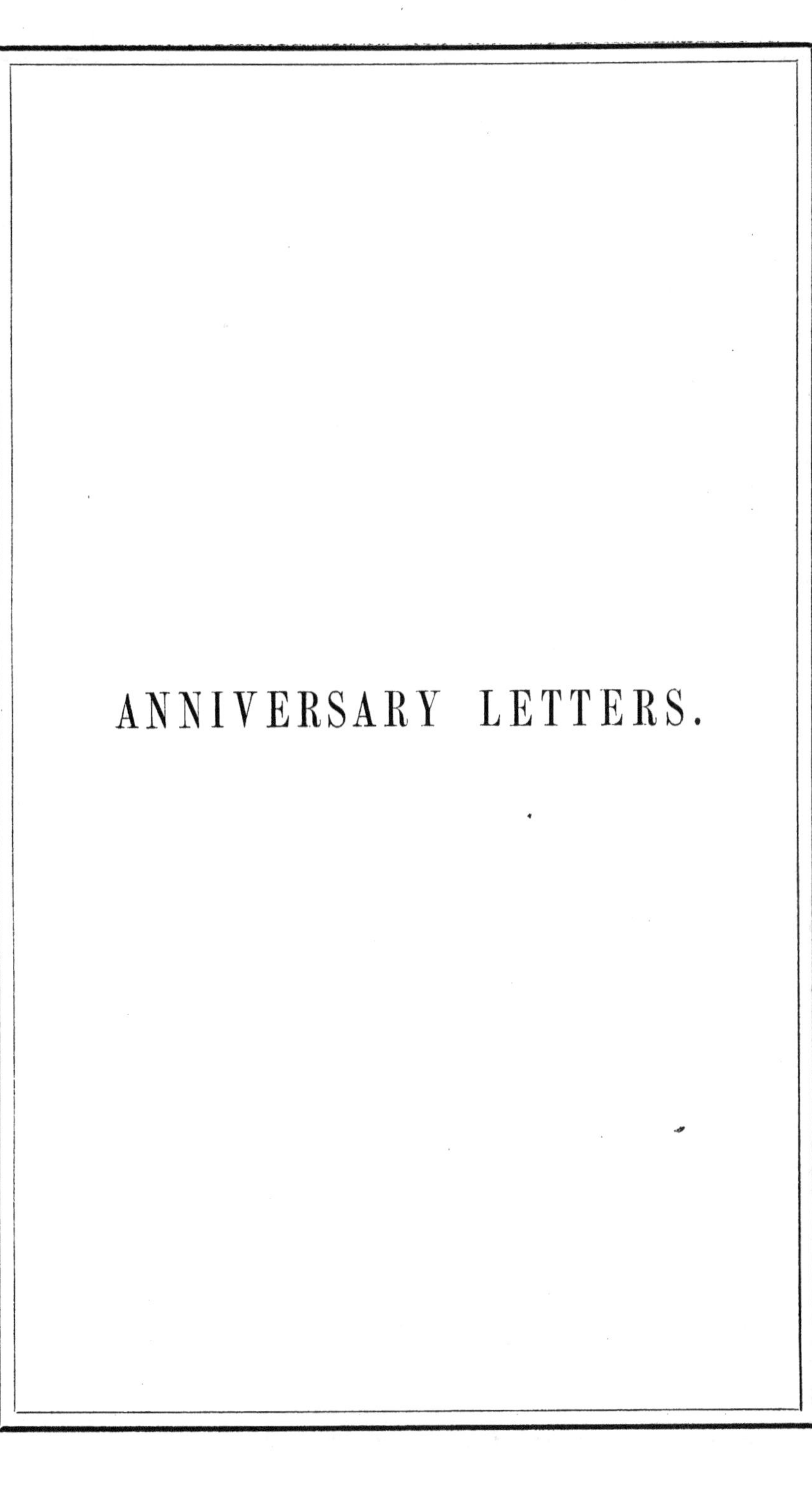

ANNIVERSARY LETTERS.

LETTERS.

FROM REV. W. W. ATTERBURY.

N. Y. Sabbath Committee Rooms,
New York, December 6th, 1869.

Dear Brethren: I very much regret my inability to accept the invitation you have kindly sent me to be present at the Twenty-Fifth Anniversary of your Church.

Brief as was my connection with the Church, it was under such circumstances as to impress very deeply all its incidents upon my memory, and to exert a most important influence upon my subsequent ministry. I came to you just from the Theological Seminary, very young in years and without experience. The Church, too, was young, and its members (many of them recent converts of a precious revival under the labors of Mr. Finney) were ardent and active. Much work was to be done outside the study and the pulpit, and to this, as promising more immediate results, I was encouraged by zealous brethren, and gave perhaps a disproportionate attention. But the influences of God's blessed Spirit were not withheld. Many were led to Christ, some of whom are with Him now, and others continue to this day. I remember well the first inquiry meeting of that winter. It had been appointed with a good deal of trepidation, but when I went there I was encouraged to find a group of eight or ten, most of whom were professors of religion in darkness, seeking light. One young man of seventeen was led that evening to decide for the Lord, and over him I rejoiced greatly as the first fruits of my ministry. Two weeks after, he came to my study with a young friend of his own age, whom he was seeking to bring to Jesus. This friend devoted himself that day to the service of his Lord as we three knelt together in prayer, and after a short but useful life among you, serving with great fidelity, and adorning the doctrine which he professed, was called home. The memory of CHARLES TYLER will long be dear to the many who knew and loved him. The other, first mentioned, the Philip who brought this Nathanael to Christ, still lives among you, as true, I trust, to the standard of the Cross, as he was to his country's flag. Many other scenes of that winter linger in my recollection, fresh and fragrant. Amid the labors of subsequent years, I have never ceased to feel a peculiar interest in, and attachment to, that company of Christ's disciples whom it was my first privilege to serve in the ministry of His Gospel.

May the smile of the Master gladden your hearts at your Anniversary, and may your beloved Church be made in years to come, as in the years that are past, a chosen instrument for promoting the honor of His Dear Name.

Faithfully yours,

W. W. ATTERBURY.

FROM HON. CHARLES G. HAMMOND.

OFFICE OF GENERAL SUP'T OF THE UNION PACIFIC R. R.
OMAHA, Neb., December 6, 1869.

DEAR BRETHREN: I am detained here, and prevented from uniting with you in the deeply-interesting occasion of your approaching anniversary, by duties which it is not possible to avoid. Accept assurances of, and present to the brethren of the Church, my profound regret that I am to lose so precious an opportunity to renew friendships which have given me great joy, and to unite with them in thanksgivings that so feeble a vine has produced so much fruit. Planted in weakness and amidst the doubts of some, against the wishes of others, surrounded by evil forebodings, and, worst of all, overwhelmed by the pity and condolence that mocked our feebleness, God graciously gave to that feebleness His strength, until, in time, you have become "two bands."

In that effort, long and arduous though it was, I did what I could, but not having done anything more than my duty, as I then viewed the ground, and as, in the retrospect, it now appears, I desire with gratitude to give all the praise to God, and to instrumentalities of His appointment, whose agency was made effective.

While I should not thus allude to myself at all, were I not forced to do so by the terms of your invitation, I must be permitted to ask you to assure the brethren and sisters who may remember me in connection with our early struggles, that I am so deeply imbued with a sense of the value of that and such organizations, upon "the foundation of the Apostles and Prophets, Jesus Christ Himself being the Chief Corner Stone," that I have not ceased to do what I could to lay their foundations. In my subsequent efforts, often amid darkness and doubt, I have not failed to behold light and gain courage from Detroit's successful achievement. Often have I called to mind the noble band of faithful ones associated there, and said, May not other bands, equally noble, be gathered and toil on to an equally assured success?

God has given success to the organization which you celebrate and to other Scriptural Congregational organizations, widely extended within these twenty-five years. He has made these organizations the happy earthly home of many of His dear ones here, and the stepping-stone to a more enduring home above.

There, my brethren and sisters, we have many dear ones, once co-laborers, now at rest, and reaping the rich rewards of their faithfulness here. I trust I need not entreat you, as you join your glad thanksgivings for all the mercies you have received for these many years, that you fail not to thank our beloved Lord that He has remembered His promises, has been faithful to His word, and taken so many to be forever with Him. Do not for a moment wish them back, but rejoice that their conflicts are past, and that they are safe "beyond the River," forever at home.

I can give but the briefest time to this note, but as I dwell for that brief time on the subject, my heart goes out after you all, and toward your contemplated meeting, and is rebellious at the self-denying certainty that I cannot go.

In cutting short what I long to utter, let me say that my wife joins truly in all that I write, and while we offer up our prayers that you may have a joyful, happy time, be filled with the Spirit, and gain strength and resolution for further conquests in the name of our dear Savior, let us ask your united remembrance of us at the "sweet hour of prayer," that we may stand up manfully for the right and meet you all in God's good time, and join that Song which is sung only in Heaven.

With Christian salutations, I am, dear brethren, yours,

C. G. HAMMOND.

FROM MYRON H. CRAFTS, ESQ.

SAN BERNARDINO, Cal., November 23, 1869.

DEAR BRETHREN: Your printed note of invitation of November 1st, to be present at the Twenty-Fifth Anniversary of the organization of the First Congregational Church at Detroit, came to hand after some delay, too late for anything to appear from me at the time of your anticipated exercises. I could not be present in person, although I can think of no one thing that would afford me more unalloyed pleasure, than to be with you on the joyous occasion.

The relations I once sustained to that Church, its individual friendships and its rich spiritual privileges are treasured up in my heart, very gratefully to you and the blessed Master, who ordained for me nearly three years of such profitable and happy fellowship.

Isolated, as I have been these many years, from such rare blessings, makes me the more deeply and fully appreciate them, and long to be with you and participate in the exercises of the occasion. But I can only be with you in spirit and tender remembrances.

May the Great Head of the Church be with you and make the days full of blessing and cheer to all hearts present. And may all the members gird themselves to do more manfully for the Master in the days that yet remain, for the advancement of His Cause and the upbuilding of His glorious Kingdom.

I am very truly yours in Christian bonds,

MYRON H. CRAFTS.

THE MEMBERSHIP

OF A

QUARTER OF A CENTURY.

LIST OF MEMBERS

From December 25, 1844, to December 25, 1869.

Avery, William T.
Avery, Olivia M.
Allen, Richard
Adams, Nancy
Adams, Laura
Atwood, Mary L.
Adams, Herbert
Atwood, H. S.
Adams, Josiah
Allen, Jane
Acker, Samuel
Acker, Betsey Ann
Adams, Sarah F.
Arnold, Henry
Arnold, Winnifred
Avery, Mary
Ackerman, Martha F.
Armstrong, Anna H.
Arnold, Mary
Adams, Thomas K.
Alden, John M.
Alden, Augusta M.
Austin, Cynthia F.
Austin, Mary H.
Austin, Joseph H.
Adams, Caroline E.
Adams, Isabel
Adams, Laura S.
Allen, Ellen
Andrews, George P.
Andrews, Sarah G.
Adams, Willie D.
Allendyce, Margaret

Baldwin, Lyman
Baldwin, Mancy
Barnard, Sherman S.
Bull, Adaline
Barnard, Mary J.
Bailey, Joseph C.
Bailey, Ann
Bates, Catharine
Brush, Amanda
Bissell, Melesent W.
Baldwin, Celia M.
Burnell, Emily J.
Blackader, John
Backus, Juliana T.
Barnum, Minerva
Beebe, Mary
Brown, Emma
Black, Catharine S.
Bushnell, Hannah H.
Brown, Emily
Barrows, Lurania
Barrows, Stephen S.
Buffum, Joshua
Buffum, Ruth H.
Braman, Cynthia
Barnard, John Q.
Barnard, Abby
Barnum, Edwin W.
Barnum, Mary E.
Bradley, Matilda
Breck, Angelina
Beattie, Martha
Beattie, Margaret
Brundage, Harvey H.
Boyd, Robert W.
Bronson, Ira
Bliss, William
Brown, Sarah
Beecher, Mary
Brooks, Caroline
Bronson, Laura E.
Bradley, Mrs. Charles
Bigelow, Mary G.
Becker, Maria L.
Beattie, Eliza
Butterfield, Harriet A.
Barnard, Emily L.
Baird, Ellen A.
Burnell, Elisabeth E.
Bradley, Artie M.
Barrett, Charles H.
Bliss, Lucy
Bliss, Frances H.
Blackader, Martha

Barnard, Mary
Bissell, Mary S.
Beattie, Robert
Brown, Maria E.
Beach, Mary N.
Bochman, Hester
Bates, Eunice E.
Baldwin, Frances
Beebe, John E.
Bull, Mary
Bronson, William H.
Burgess, Henry A.
Burgess, Julia E.
Bostwick, Henry E.
Bartley, Mary E.
Bartley, Sarah E.
Bradner, Addie S.
Bates, Jane
Burgess, Mary P.
Bigelow, Joseph E.
Baker, Henry E.
Baker, Emily P.
Barnum, Lucretia S.
Bostwick, Sophia A.
Beebe, Abigail
Beattie, Martha
Butler, Hannah
Bates, Frederic D.
Burroughs, Louisa L.
Bates, Joanna
Baker, Henry S.
Baldwin, John A.
Bellows, Jane A.
Butler, Emma M.
Bigelow, Charles P.
Beard, Robert R.
Bell, Daniel P.
Bell, Clarissa E.
Brown, Sylvia
Burr, William H.
Butler, Charles W.
Brooks, Margaret
Brooks, Mary

Crane, James G.
Crane, Mary A.
Cook, William
Cook, Marietta P.
Curtis, Charles
Craig, Jane E.
Case, Sidney C.
Clark, Susan A.

Cowles, Rhoda	Clough, Eliza A.
Church, Philetus S.	Case, Caroline M.
Church, Elisabeth D.	Case, Marcia L. C.
Coit, Samuel	Crossman, Martha
Cushing, Martha A.	Crossman, Caroline
Coe, Israel	Crafts, Myron H.
Crane, Louisa M.	Craig, Phidelia A.
Coit, Mary E.	Carrier, Frances M.
Coe, Huldah	Crossman, Lucy
Christie, Joseph A.	Cooper, Ellen E.
Christie, Judith	Carlisle, Frederic
Coe, Cornelia	Carlisle, Charlotte
Cushing, Charles S.	Chaney, Lucien C.
Common, George	Curtis, Lewis M.
Common, Jane	Curtis, Charlotte S.
Coe, Sarah M.	Clark, Eliza D.
Coe, Adelaide E.	Clark, Marietta L.
Campbell, Maria	Carrier, Mary E.
Chaffin, Patience B.	Cushing, Lizzie S.
Carpenter, J. H.	Cheyne, George
Chase, John A.	Clark, Gardner K.
Cook, Ann	Carrier Albert E.
Conklin, Anna	Cochrane, Sarah A.
Campbell, Maria T.	Clark, George H.
Crossman, Charles	Clark, Flora
Carpenter, Alida	Coit, Mary R.
Clark, Edwin M.	Clark, James

Cook, Celestia A.
Chubb, O. P.
Chubb, Mrs. O. P.
Clapp, Samuel H.
Clapp, Hannah H.
Clark, Lydia M.
Carver, David
Carver, Jane T.
Clark, Mary E.
Clark, Nancy
Colburn, William B.
Colburn, Betsey M.
Carey, Sarah E.
Carey, Alice A.
Colwell, Mrs. M. L.
Cook, Mary A.
Clark, Olive J.
Carew, Charlotte

Dort, Mary
Donaldson, Agnes
Duncklee, Mary C.
Dwight, Phœbe
Dwight, Miriam
Duncklee, William S.
Duncklee, Lydia L.
Dimmick, Electa
Davis, William W.
Duncklee, Hubbard H.
Draper, Minerva L.
Davis, Nancy
Doremus, Harriet J.
Davis, Samuel
Davis, Caroline
Damai, Cornelius
Damai, Sarah
Doremus, William T.
Davidson, Ellen
Duncan, Louisa
Dilman, Mrs. Ira
Duncan, Harriet
Dolson, Lura
Davis, Mary
Durand, Emily M.
Durand, Emma C.

Edwards, William R.
Everett, Jane
Everett, Amelia
Edwards, Elisabeth
Elmore, Almira
Edwards, Catharine,

EDWARDS, ELEANOR
EDWARDS, MARY P. L.

EDWARDS, MARIANNE
EDWARDS, DAVID

FISHER, CATHARINE
FOWLER, STEPHEN
FISHER, MARY
FROST, MAHLON S.
FERGUSON, SARAH
FOOTE, PHŒBE
FISHER, ESTHER
FARRAND, RHODA E.
FITCH, EDWARD D.
FISHER, GALEN M.
FISHER, SUSAN
FLOWERS, Mrs. ——
FITCH, ELISABETH A.
FOLSOM, SARAH A.

FARRAND, BETHUEL C.
FARRAND, HELEN W.
FARRELL, CATHARINE H.
FARRELL, THOMAS
FARRELL, CATHARINE
FISHER, SUSAN T.
FULLER, AMELIA
FLORENCE, MARY A.
FOSTER, Mrs. JOSEPH
FOSTER, Mrs. JOSEPH Jr.
FREELAND, Rev. SAM'L M.
FREELAND, ELISABETH L.
FERRY, FANNY B.

GREEN, IRENE E.
GILBERT, ANN C.
GILBERT, HARRIET L.
GIEKIE, WALTER D.
GREEN, CALVIN H.
GREEN, ESTHER E.
GREEN, JAMES H.
GILBERT, GEORGE
GRACE, WILLIAM

GARDINER, MARGARETTA M.
GRIGGS, STEPHEN
GRAY, EMILY R.
GRAHAM, ELIZA A.
GRIFFITH, JOHN H.
GORE, HARRIET L.
GLEASON, AMELIA
GILBERT, MARIETTA
GRIGGS, L. LAVONNE

GEORGE, NELSON
GEORGE, ALTHEA
GUILE, JAMES M.
GUILE, ANN E.
GRISWOLD, THADDEUS
GUNNING, WILLIAM C.
GUNNING, Mrs. WILLIAM C.
GRIGGS, LUCY E.
GREEN, GEORGE S.
GRIGGS, FRANCES E.
GEER, ROSETTA
GILMORE, LENORA S.
GRIFFITH, ELLA M.
GIAUQUE, JAMES D.
GILMORE, GEORGE N.
GILMORE, SARAH
GIAUQUE BESSIE A.

HAMMOND, MARY JANE
HANSON, STEPHEN T.
HANSON, MARY J.
HAMMOND, Rev. HENRY L.
HAMMOND, CHARLES G.
HAMMOND, CHARLOTTE B.
HOAG, H. P.
HOWARD, CHARLES
HOWARD, LYDIA
HENRY, HUGH
HENRY, LOUISA
HART, JAMES
HART, SARAH
HAMMOND, SERENO C.
HAMMOND, RACHEL J.
HOWARD, JOHN E.
HOLMAN, ELISABETH A.
HOWARD, STEPHEN
HOLMAN, HARRIET
HORNE, MARGARET
HOLMES, EMELINE W.
HIBBARD, ISAIAH W.
HIBBARD, Mrs. IRENE S.
HOLMES, ALICE
HAWLEY, LUCY A.
HIBBARD, HANNAH S.
HAWLEY, CAROLINE B.
HITTEL, SAMUEL
HITTEL, AMELIA C.
HOLMES, GEORGE W.
HALL, EDMUND
HALL, EMELINE C.
HINSDALE, EDWIN C.
HINSDALE, ELLEN J.
HINSDILL, CHARLOTTE
HOWARD, CATHARINE A.

Holmes, Silas M.
Holmes, Eliza A.
Henderson, Sarah,
Harris, Eliza P.
Hale, Mrs. E. J.
Henry, D. Farrand
Hunter, Theodore
Hall, Charles
Hall, Sarah
Hall, Eliza
Hall, George E.
Hamlyn, William
Hoyt, Harriet M.
Holmes, Jabish
Holmes, Lydia
Higgins, Mary T.
Hickok, William H.
Harter, Catharine
Hollywood, Theodosia
Holman, Sullivan
Holman, Mrs. S.
Hebbard, Charles B.
Hibbard, Irene S.
Henderson, John
Henderson, Rachel
Hall, Sarah M.
Hammond, Isabel T.
Henderson, Clara L.
Hammond, Sereno P.
Henderson, James F.
Hubbell, Mrs. N. J.
Holbrook, Hattie B.
Howard, Alfred
Howe, Sarah
Holdsworth, James
Henry, William G.
Henry, Huldanah S.
Henry, Faydelia S.
Henry, Aurelia S.
Hepburn, James H.
Hepburn, Georgie
Howe, Mrs. G. W.

Ingersoll, Emily M.

Jones, Mary J.
James, John
Jones, Mary A.
Jones, Jane
Jones, Richard L.
James, Keturah C.

JONES, CHARLES S.	JOHNSON, ELISABETH
JONES, EDMUND D.	JONES, ANGELINE M.
JONES, FANNY E.	JONES, MARY J.
JONES, ADALINE	JONES, DAVID
JONES, REBECCA M.	
KIMBALL, MARY J.	KELLOGG, EMILY C.
KING, ROBERT W.	KELLEY, GEORGE B.
KING, ELISABETH	KELLEY, AMELIA F.
KITCHEL, REV. HARVEY D.	KINNEY, EURETTA A.
KITCHEL, ANNA	KITCHEL, COURTNEY S.
KING, BERIAH	KANADY, WILLIAM S.
KING, MARY A.	KANADY, CALISTA M.
KNIGHT, ELLEN J.	KANADY, SARAH C.
KERR, POLLY P.	KING, C. FRANCES
KITCHEL, CORNELIUS L.	KANADY, HARRIET B.
KNIBLO, CLARA	KNAPP, AVERY
LUDDEN, SILAS	LEE, HENRY H.
LAING, EDWARD S.	LAPHAM, MARIA A.
LITTLE, ANN	LILLYBRIDGE, MINERVA
LOW, LUCY	LOOSE, JOHN F.
LANE, MINOT T.	LAWRENCE, GERTRUDE M.
LANE, RUTH F.	LAPHAM, NOAH D.
LANE, GEORGE M.	LOWE, EUGENE S.
LEMCKE, SEVILLA	LYLE, SUSAN
LATHROP, SOLOMON JR.	LATHROP, WILLIAM H.

LEONARD, JOHN J.
LEE, Mrs. H. H.
LAIBLE, MARY L.

McDOWELL, SARAH A.
MADDOCK, JABEZ
MATHER, LUCY P.
McLEOD, ANN
McKIBBIN, ELIZA J.
MATTISON, JOHN
MOTHERWELL, ISABELLA
McLANE, ISABELLA
MITCHELL, MARY
McCRAE, JOHN
McLEAN, JAMES
MILLER, FRANCES
McCRAE, ELISABETH
MARTIN, HENRY
MORSE, E. CORREY
MAY, JOHN
MORSE, JERUSHA A.
MELLUS, CECILIA
MARSHALL, ADAM
MARSHALL, MARGARET
McPHERSON, ELIZA
MUNROE, HULDAH A.
MURRAY, FRANCES C.
MORSE, JERUSHA A.
MORSE, MARY L.
MORSE, ELIZA S.
MOTT, Mrs. J. T.
McGUIRE, MARGARET
MOTT, MARIA F.
McMANMAN, ELISABETH S.
MESSINGER, MARY A.
MESSINGER, M. JANE
MESSINGER, H. FRANK
MESSINGER, MELVINA G.
MARCY, LORENZO J.
McKENZIE, D.
McKENZIE, Mrs. D.
MILLER, ELISABETH
MESSINGER, HARRIET J.
MATHER, DELIA
MOIR, Mrs. WILLIAM
McBANE, WILLIAM
MILLER, MAGGIE E.
MOORE, IDA A.
MUNGER, SIMEON
MUNGER, ELLEN J.

Mellus, Christian
Millard, George
Mead, Samuel P.
Mead, Elisabeth
Monds, Hettie
Morris, George
Morris, Aurelia
Madison, Abigail
Messinger, Martha E.
Morse, Perley
Marshall, Rachel G.
Munger, Alonzo P.
Moir, Jennie M.
Maynard, Ellen J.
Maynard, William
Mowrey, Christian
Murphy, Thomas
Murphy, Maria
Montgomery, Emma V.
Morse, Mary W.
McKay, James A.
McKay, Charlotte H.

Nall, James, Jr.
Nall, Henry
Noble, Daniel
Noble, Julia B.
Nash, Deborah
Nall, Frances
Niles, Martha
Noble, William
Newhall, Eliza
Nall, Charles J.
Noble, Margaretta
Nall, Arthur A.
Nall, Isabella F.
Nall, Matilda L.
Niles, Jane A.
Niles, Charles
Nichols, Clorinda B.

Osborn, Sarah E.
Oven, John
Oven, George
O'Callaghan, Olivia C.
Orr, Samuel A.
Otis, Mary
Oxnard, John E.
Oxnard, Maria H. P.

Powell, A. C.
Parsons, Philo
Parsons, Ann E.
Parshall, Cornelia
Purdy, William
Partridge, Timothy L.
Payne, Douglass
Purdy, Robert
Purdy, Mrs. Robert
Purdy, Mary
Purdy, Harriet A.
Park, Sarah
Patchen, Squire W.
Patchen, Abby B.
Perkins, Asa E.
Parrish, Lee
Parrish, Hannah J.
Porter, Eliza G.
Perkins, Sarah A.
Perrin, Hiram M.
Perrin, Eveline
Powell, Celestia A.
Pert, Elisabeth
Pritchard, Walter
Penfield, David O.
Penfield, Sarah
Pritchard, Timothy
Pierce, Albert D.
Parker, Delia A.
Palmer, Calvin D.
Palmer, Ervin
Preston, Julia E.
Prouty, Catharine
Phillips, E. D.
Porter, C. Helen
Palmer, Emma L.
Penfield, Cornelia
Pearl, Harriet L.
Prouty, William
Pierce, Caroline B.
Pease, Thomas H.
Penfield, Sarah E.
Purdy, Mary
Purdy, Joseph W.
Parker, Edwin
Purdy, Ella J.

Raymond, Francis
Raymond, Ruth
Raymond, James M.
Rolefson, Mary
Rolefson, Anna
Robertson, James

Robertson, Janet
Read, Elisabeth, A.
Rice, Mary
Raymond, Charlotte
Redfield, Alex. H.
Rice, Betsey W.
Rice, Mrs. Mary
Rice, Mary
Rice, Anna W.
Rice, Harriet
Randolph, Jane
Robinson, Martha
Robinson, Mary
Richardson, David M.
Richardson, Ellen L.
Randolph, Merritt
Robertson, Ellen
Robinson, Ann E.
Robinson, John
Russell, Emily L.
Richardson, Levi
Richardson, Jane B.
Robinson, Martha
Robinson, Ruth
Roberts, Ann
Rose, Melissa
Randall, Freeman R.
Randolph, Emily
Robertson, Margaret
Richardson, Laura

Stroud, Mary A.
Sackett, Sophronia
Stebbins, Noadiah D.
Stebbins, Emily
Stevens, Amos 2d
Steevens, Sears
Smith, Ralph C.
Smith, Jane
Sumner, Frederic M.
Sumner, Elisabeth E.
Shaw, Elisabeth T.
Selden, Laura A.
Sirard, Louis
Sirard, Mrs. L.
Swift, Mary A. B.
Stetson, Turner
Stetson, Sarah
Silsbee, Charles E.
Silsbee, Mary E.
Scott, Lydia
Smith, Mrs. H. C.
Silsbee, Caroline E.

Swift, Frederic W.
Simpson, Margaret
Stevens, William F.
Sunbury, Heman B.
Sunbury, Mrs. H. B.
Stephens, Anna
Stevens, Oren
Stoddard, Olivia
Sprague, Mary E.
Stevens, Margaret
Stebbins, Dwight
Stebbins, Edward
Stebbins, Theodore
Smith, Phila J.
Smith, Esther A.
Sheldon, B. M.
Sheldon, Electa M.
Story, H. G.
Story, Mrs. H. G.
Sanford, Thomas
Sanford, Mary
Seymour, George G.
Smith, Oliver B.
Smith, Mary E.
Sabine, Alfred
Sabine, Martha
Selden Joseph G.
Sabin, Orrin T.
Stewart, Sarah
Shourds, Phœbe E.
Silsbee, Sarah C.
Standish, Susan
Safford, Charles L.
Safford, Mary
Scripps, James E.
Standart, Mary M.
Stevens, Betsey
Shephard, Helen N.
Sawyer, Ellen
Sabin, Susan
Safford, Lucretia
Sabine, Susan
Sabine, Mary A.
Sheaver, Lavinia
Seymour, Francis H.
Silsbee, James D.
Stevenson George E.
Smith, Emma
Stocking, William
Sheldon, Nettie
Swift, Henry F.
Swift, Angelina B.
Shepard, Ellen A.

Tyler, Elisha
Tyler, Mary G.
Town, Reuben
Town, Mary H.
Tyler, Rowland G.
Town, Semantha A.
Tuttle, Nancy
Tait, Elisabeth
Tyler, Charles C.
Tyler, Susannah
Tibbetts, Helen
Tyler, Olive
Thompson, Elisabeth
Taylor, Nathaniel T.
Taylor, Laura N.
Taylor, Sarah E.
Taylor, Frances M.
Tillman, Mary
Tyler, Moses C.
Thomas, Eleanor
Thompson, Rev. Orrin C.
Thompson, Mrs. Alice
Ten Eyck, John M.
Ten Eyck, Elisabeth
Tate, Mary
Thompson, Laura C.
Todd, James
Thompson, Alice
Tarbell, Lydia B.
Tyler, Edward S.
Trowbridge, Luther S.
Tucker, George
Tarbell, Frances J.
Taylor, Frank D.
Trowbridge, Harriet A.
Tyler, Elisabeth C.
Thompson, Orrin C. Jr.
Taylor, N. Terry
Torrence, James

Utley, Kate

Van Valen, Mary
Van Valen, Sarah
Voorheis, Jacob E.
Voorheis, Harriet K.
Vandermeer, Martha L.
Vandermeer, Abram J.

VAN HOUTEN, HARRIET R.
VAN TASSELL, FANNY
VAN TINE, ALMIRA

WARNER, ROBERT W.
WARNER, CAROLINE A.
WELLS, CALVIN Jr.
WHITCOMB, LUCIA A.
WATKINS, JOHN
WATKINS, NANCY
WATKINS, MARY J.
WALCOTT, ALBERT
WALCOTT, MARTHA
WHITTEMORE, GIDEON O.
WHITTEMORE, HARRIET
WHITTEMORE, JAMES O.
WHITCOMB, JAMES M.
WOODBRIDGE, DUDLEY B.
WATSON, RUBENA
WALLACE, NANCY
WALCOTT, JULIA
WHEATON, Mrs. HORACE
WILKINS, MARIA
WATSON, JANE
WALCOTT, GEORGE
WAGNER, CHARLOTTE
WELLS, BARENT V. B.
WALKER, MARY A.
WIGHT, NANCY M.
WYMAN, JULIA A.
WARNER, WILLIAM
WARNER, HARRIET B.
WEYMOUTH, MARY A.
WILNER, AUGUSTA
WANZER, SARAH H.
WIGHT, EDWARD H.
WARNER, HELEN
WARNER, HARRIET
WOODLEY, J. W.
WOODLEY, Mrs. J. W.
WALKER, H. W.
WARNER, FRANCES R.
WHITE, THOMAS
WATSON, HORACE C.
WATSON, ELISABETH A.
WATSON, SARAH A.
WALKER, Mrs. W.
WARNER, FRANCES S.
WILKINS, JULIA
WALKER, HARRIET
WILKES, JOHN A.
WILKES, ALICE
WARD, SARAH R.
WATSON, ANNA D.

Whitwood, Caroline E.
Williams, David
Webb, J. G.
Waring, Merritt J.
Waring, Anna W.
Wheaton, William W.
Weston, Andrew J.
Walker, Charles I.
Wheaton, Maria L.
Wright, Frances C.
Woodruff, W. Warren
Welch, Joseph A.
Wilkins, Alvan
Wilkins, Charlotte
Wilkins, Fanny
Wormer, Grover S.
Woodbridge, Martha J.
Wheaton, Alida M.
Watson, Andrew
Warner, Martha S.
Watson, Isabella
Wilkins, Alice G.
Williams, Kate C.
Woolsey, Fidelia
Watson, Joseph E.
Weed, Arthur B.
Weed, Porter L.
Weed, Carrie L.
Williams, Morys L.
Wolcott, Rev. William
Williams, Richard P.

LIST OF MEMBERS

CONSTITUTING THE FIRST CONGREGATIONAL CHURCH DEC. 25, 1869.*

ADAMS, NANCY
ACKER, SAMUEL
ACKER, BETSEY A.
AVERY, MARY
ADAMS, THOMAS K.
ADAMS, SARAH F.
ADAMS, LAURA S.
ADAMS, WILLIE D.
ALLEN, RUTH
ANGELL, SARAH M.
ALDEN, JOHN M.
ALDEN, AUGUSTA M.
ADAMS, CAROLINE E.
ANDREWS, GEORGE P.
ANDREWS, SARAH G.
ALLENDYCE, MARGARET

BALDWIN, LYMAN
BALDWIN, MANCY
BALDWIN, JOHN A.
BARNARD, SHERMAN S.
BARNARD, MARY J.
BARNARD, EMILY L.
BISSELL, MELESENT W.
BLACKADER, JOHN
BLACKADER, MARTHA
BOSTWICK, HENRY E.
BOSTWICK, SOPHIA A.
BATES, JANE
BAKER, HENRY E.
BAKER, EMILY P.
BEEBE, ABIGAIL
BURROUGHS, LOUISA L.

---

*For list of members constituting the Church, December 25, 1844, see page 32.

Backus, Juliana T.
Bushnell, Hannah H.
Brooks, Caroline
Brooks, Mary
Bellows, Jane A.
Bell, Daniel P.
Bell, Clarissa E.
Becker, Maria L.

Cooke, William
Cooke, Marietta P.
Case, Sidney C.
Clark, Susan A.
Cowles, Rhoda
Coe, Adelaide E.
Crossman, Charles
Crossman, Martha
Crossman, Caroline
Crossman, Lucy
Craig, Phidelia A.
Carpenter, Alida
Clark, E. Miner
Clark, Mary
Clough, Eliza A.
Case, Caroline M.
Carlisle, Frederic
Carlisle, Charlotte
Clement, Anna
Chaney, Lucien C.
Clark, Eliza D.
Clark, Flora
Clark, James
Clark, Nancy
Carver, David
Colburn, Betsey M.
Carey, Sarah E.
Carey, Alice A.
Colwell, Mrs. M. L.
Cook, Mary A.
Clark, Olive J.
Carew, Charlotte

Duncklee, William S.
Duncklee, Lydia L.
Davidson, Ellen
Dolson, Emily J.
Duncan, Louisa
Durand, Emily M.
Day, Mary R.

Elmore, Almira

Fisher, Esther	Fields, Sarah A.
Farrell, Catharine H.	Foster, Clara
Farrell, Catharine	Foster, Mrs. Joseph
Gilbert, George	Griffith, John H.
Gilbert, Ann C.	Griffith, Ella M.
Griggs, Stephen	Gore, Harriet L.
Griggs, Lucy E.	Gilmore, George N.
Griggs, Frances E.	Gilmore, Sarah
Gray, Emily R.	
Hammond, Rachel J.	Holmes, Lydia
Hammond, Sereno P.	Holman, Sullivan
Holmes, Emeline W.	Holman, Mrs. S.
Hawley, Lucy A.	Hebbard, Charles B.
Hall, Edmund	Holbrook, Hattie B.
Hall, Emeline C.	Howard, Alfred
Hinsdale, Edwin C.	Howard, Caroline B.
Hinsdale, Ellen J.	Holdsworth, James
Hinsdill, Charlotte	Henry, William G.
Holmes, Silas M.	Henry, Huldanah S.
Holmes, Eliza A.	Henry, Faydelia S.
Henry, D. Farrand	Henry, Aurelia S.
Hall, Eliza	Hepburn, James H.
Hall, Sarah	Hepburn, Georgie
Hoyt, Harriet M.	Howe, Mrs. G. W.
Holmes, Jabish	Howe, Sarah

Hibbard, Sarah M.
Hickok, William H.
Harter, Catharine M.
Hackett, Abby
Haskell, Celestia A.

James, John
Jones, Edmund D.
Jones, Mary J.
Jones, David
Jones, Martha
Jerome, Delia

King, Robert W.
King, Elisabeth
King, C. Frances
Kinney, Euretta A.
Klein, Sevilla

Lane, Minot T.
Lane, George M.
Lane, Mary P. L.
Lathrop, William H.
Leonard, John J.
Laible, Mary L.
*Lawrence, Mary A.

Motherwell, Isabella
McCrae, John
McCrae, Elisabeth
Miller, Frances
Mellus, Christian
Mellus, Cecilia
Munroe, Huldah A.
Mott, Mrs. J. T.
Mott, Maria F.
McKenzie, D.
McKenzie, Mrs. D.
Moir, Mrs. William
Moir, Jennie M.
Maynard, William
Mowrey, Christian
Murphy, Thomas

*Accidentally omitted from the preceding list.

McGuire, Margaret	Montgomery, Emma V.
McManman, Elisabeth S.	Morse, Mary W.
Messinger, Mary A.	McKay, James A.
Messinger, M. Jane	McKay, Charlotte H.
Nall, Charles J.	Niles, Jane A.
Nall, Matilda L.	Niles, Charles
Nall, Arthur A.	Nichols, Clorinda B.
Nall, Ida A.	
Oxnard, John E.	Oxnard, Maria H. P.
Parsons, Philo	Palmer, Addie S.
Parsons, Ann E.	Prouty, Catharine
Partridge, Timothy L.	Prouty, William
Partridge, Minerva	Porter, C. Helen
Parrish, Lee	Pease, Thomas H.
Parrish, Hannah J.	Purdy, Mary
Porter, Eliza G.	Purdy, Joseph W.
Pierce, Albert D.	Purdy, Ella J.
Pierce, Caroline B.	Parker, Edwin
Palmer, Calvin D.	Pond, Harriet L.
Raymond, Francis	Robinson, Martha
Raymond, Ruth	Robinson, Mary
Raymond, Gertrude M.	Richardson, David M.
Randolph, Jane	Richardson, Laura

ROBERTSON, JAMES
ROBERTSON, JANET
ROBERTSON, MARGARET
RUSSELL, EMILY L.
ROYS, ELIZA J.

STEEVENS, SEARS
SMITH, RALPH C.
SMITH, JANE
SMITH, EMMA
SWIFT, FREDERIC W.
SWIFT, MARY A. B.
SANFORD, THOMAS
STETSON, SARAH
SMITH, Mrs. H. C.
STEWART, SARAH
SCRIPPS, JAMES E.
SCRIPPS, HARRIET J.
STANDART, MARY M.
SHEAVER, LAVINIA
STARR, EMILY C.
SUTTON, JOANNA B.
STOCKING, WILLIAM
SHELDON, NETTIE
SWIFT, HENRY F.
SWIFT, ANGELINA B.
SHEPARD, ELLEN A.

TUTTLE, NANCY
THOMPSON, Rev. ORRIN C.
THOMPSON, ALICE
TARBELL, LYDIA B.
TARBELL, FRANCES J.
TORRENCE, JAMES

WOODBRIDGE, DUDLEY B.
WOODBRIDGE, MARTHA J.
WELLS, BARENT V. B.
WHEATON, WM. W.
WHEATON, FANNY
WHEATON, ADELLA M.
WALKER, CHARLES I.
WILKINS, ALVAN
WILKINS, CHARLOTTE
WILKINS, ALICE G.
WYMAN, JULIA A.
WHITE, EDWARD H.
WRIGHT, FRANCES C.
WARNER, FRANCES S.
WARNER, HELEN
WARNER, HARRIET
WARNER, MARTHA S.
WHITE, THOMAS
WATSON, ANDREW
WATSON, ISABELLA
WILLIAMS, MORYS L.
WILLIAMS, KATE C.
WILLIAMS, RICHARD P.

LIST OF MEMBERS

DISMISSED TO, AND ORIGINALLY CONSTITUTING, THE SECOND CONGREGATIONAL CHURCH.

Allen, Ellen E.
Arnold, Winnifred
Arnold, Mary

Bronson, William H.
Bronson, Laura E. L.
Bronson, Mary
Barrett, Charles H.
Barrett, Frances M.
Bliss, Lucy
Burr, William H.
Baker, Henry S.
Butler, Emma M.
Butler, Hannah B.

Cochrane, Sarah A.
Carrier, Albert E.
Carrier, Irene S.
Carrier, Mary E.
Carrier, Frances M.
Cushing, Charles S.
Cushing, Martha A.
Cushing, Lizzie E.
Cheyne, George
Curtis, Lewis M.
Curtis, Charlotte S.
Curtis, Charles H.
Clark, Ellen

Dolson, Lura
Duncan, Harriet S.

Edwards, Eleanor
Edwards, Marianne

Edwards, David
Edwards, Elisabeth
Edwards, Catharine

Foster, Henrietta
Fisher, Catharine
Fisher, Mary
Freeland, Rev. Samuel M.
Freeland, Elisabeth L.

Grant, Amanda
Gleason, Amelia
Geer, Rosetta
Gilmore, Lenora S.

Horne, Margaret
Henderson, John
Henderson, Rachel
Henderson, Clara L.
Henderson, James F.
Hubbell, Mrs. N. J.

Kelley, George B.
Kelley, Amelia F.
Kanady, William S.
Kanady, Calista M.
Kanady, Sarah C.
Kanady, Harriet B.
Kanady, Martha E.

Lapham, Noah D.
Lapham, Maria A.
Lowe, Eugene S.

Miller, Elisabeth
Miller, Maggie E.
Maynard, Emily
Munger, Simeon
Munger, Alonzo P.
Munger, Melissa
Munger, Ellen J.
*Mott, Maria F.

Newhall, Eliza

Penfield, David O.
Penfield, Sarah
Penfield, Cornelia
Penfield, Sarah E.
Palmer, Ervin
Palmer, Emma L.
Preston, Julia E.

*Subsequently re-dismissed to the First Congregational Church.

Randolph, Merritt
Randolph, Emily
Rose, Melissa
Randall, Freeman R.

Sabine, Alfred
Sabine, Martha
Silsbee, Charles E.
Silsbee, Mary E.
Silsbee, Sarah C.
Silsbee, James D.
Scott, Lydia
Sabin, Orrin T.
Sabin, Laura A.
Shephard, Helen N.
Seymour, Francis H.
Stevenson George E.

Terry, Fanny B.
Taylor, Laura N.
Taylor, N. Terry
Taylor, Frank D.
Taylor, Phœbe E.

Utley, Kate

Vandermeer, Abram J.
Vandermeer, Martha L.

Watson, Horace C.
Watson, Elisabeth A.
Watson, Sarah A.
Watson, Anna D.
Watson, Joseph E.
Wormer, Grover S.
Wormer, Maria C.
Woolsey, Delia E.
Weston, Andrew J.
Weston, Harriet
Weymouth, Mary A.
Weed, Porter L.
Weed, Caroline M.
Weed, Arthur B.
*Williams, Kate C.

*Subsequently re-dismissed to the First Congregational Church.

www.ingramcontent.com/pod-product-compliance
Lightning Source LLC
LaVergne TN
LVHW021406110826
845150LV00007B/1806

* 9 7 8 1 4 2 5 5 1 1 8 7 6 *